Praise for *The Way of the Psychic Heart*

"A must read for beginners who want to open their intuition and psychic abilities."

—Mary J. Getten, author of the Nautilus
Award-winning book, *Communicating with Orcas*

"This deeply thoughtful book provides the reader with the foundation necessary to not only strengthen heart-centered psychic abilities, but to thrive in over-all wellbeing…[it's] a joy to read and is destined to become a psychic's best companion."

—Elaine Clayton, artist, reiki master,
and author of *Making Marks*

"With the keys the author presents in this highly informative and enlightening book, anyone can unlock the door to a more intuitive way of knowing and living, as well as develop psychic skills that will allow for a more balanced and enjoyable life."

—Marie D. Jones, author of *Destiny vs. Choice*

THE WAY OF THE
PSYCHIC HEART

Mercree Media

About the Author

Chad Mercree has had psychic experiences for as long as he can remember. He has spent many years independently exploring his psychic gifts. He holds a bachelor of science degree in natural resources management from Grand Valley State University in Michigan. Chad devotes his free time to practicing meditation, yoga, and the martial arts, and teaching, writing, and filmmaking. He lives in Naples, Florida.

You can reach hin at chadmercree.com.

THE WAY OF THE
PSYCHIC HEART

Developing Your Spiritual
Gifts in the Everyday World

CHAD MERCREE

Llewellyn Publications
Woodbury, Minnesota

FIRST EDITION
First Printing, 2014

Cover art: iStockphoto.com/19043244/kirr
Cover design by Ellen Lawson
Interior art: iStockphoto.com/19043244/kirr

Llewellyn Publications is a registered trademark of Llewellyn Worldwide Ltd.

Library of Congress Cataloging-in-Publication Data
Mercree, Chad, 1970–
  The way of the psychic heart : developing your spiritual gifts in the
everyday world / Chad Mercree. — First Edition.
      pages   cm
  Includes bibliographical references.
  ISBN 978-0-7387-4040-9
1. Spiritual life. 2. Psychic ability. I. Title.
  BL624.M455 2014
  133.8—dc23
                                                                2014001933

Llewellyn Publications
A Division of Llewellyn Worldwide Ltd.
2143 Wooddale Drive
Woodbury, MN 55125-2989
www.llewellyn.com

Printed in the United States of America

Contents

Part I: Foundation

Part II: Learning to See with the Three Pillars

Part III: Learning to Listen

Part IV: Being Psychic

List of Exercises

This book is dedicated to all of my spiritual guides and teachers,
and to my wife, who has been such an inspiration to me.

Introduction

Spiritual Gifts Are Real

The world is full of magic things,
patiently waiting for our senses to grow sharper.
—W. B. YEATS

You've picked up this book, so chances are you already believe in the possibility that there are people in the world who are psychic. Psychics have different quirky traits hard to pigeonhole; some see auras, others see the future. There are some who claim to see ghosts, while others talk to animals. Have you ever had a similar experience? If so, you're not alone. Many of us know someone personally who has had a psychic experience, often more than one. We trust them. They're normal everyday people who would never lie about such things.

I grew up blessed with many psychic abilities. I had dreams of future events. I could hear people's thoughts and feel their emotions. I saw ghosts and other types of spirits, and these experiences didn't frighten me. My parents were interested in the concept of extrasensory perception, our so-called sixth sense, and played guessing games with my sister and me when we were very young. My father had a game called Flat-'Em Down, in which we guessed whether a card was a black or red suit, a number or a face. At three and four years old, these were fun, simple games, but the experience helped make the whole concept of magic and psychic abilities seem normal to me. I remember being so mad at my sister when I was a little kid because she always knew what I got her for Christmas! Her intuition was potent.

Despite those early games, as my abilities organically unfolded and I paid attention to them more and more, I never talked about my abilities. I kept to myself about my experiences until I met another young psychic in junior high school.

In 1987, Shirley MacLaine's made-for-TV movie *Out on a Limb* aired. *Out on a Limb* featured a lot of things I had experienced, and it brought psychic abilities to the public eye in a mainstream way. After I saw her movie, I started talking more about my experiences with my family but still kept quiet about my abilities in public. I grew up in a very conservative, religious part of the country, where people literally thought you were going to burn in hell for having a personal relationship with God, for not going to church, or for doing anything kooky. Folks like me were soon to experience an eternal barbecue in hell. I personally thought they were a bit melodramatic, but I didn't argue.

In the summer between high school and college, I spent many hours walking eighty acres of pristine land my family owned in western Michigan. We called the land "The Property." At one time we lived right next door to the land, on an old farmhouse in the country. It was the house where years earlier my sister and I had played Flat-'Em Down with our father. However, at the time of this summer we had already lived in a nearby city for several years and were generally too busy to visit the pristine land as we once did. Everybody had become wrapped up in school, friends, work, and the general hustle and bustle of city living.

I was amazed at the vast diversity of plants and animals I rediscovered at the Property. All of my psychic abilities were heightened there and allowed my intuition to guide me through the forests, meadows, swamps, and bogs that were home to hundreds of different species of plants and animals. I felt my intuition pull me deeper into the forest and I followed, until I stood in front of an old aspen tree. I looked up and saw an incredibly obese raccoon sleeping on a flat limb high up in the tree. Napping seemed like a good idea, so I sat at the base of the tree and rested.

When I awoke, the raccoon was gone. I looked around and saw many layers of auras and energy in the forest. My intuition guided me to look around the other side of the tree. There I discovered a most unusual looking plant with olive-gray leaves embedded with a white checkerboard pattern. The plant was blooming and had curious little white flowers as well. I'd never seen such a plant before and decided to look it up when I got home. I discovered the plant was an orchid, a type of plant I had only heard of as living in tropical areas.

I was so shocked to discover an orchid growing in Michigan that I switched my major from anthropology and art courses at the college to environmental science. I couldn't believe such an extraordinary plant had gone unnoticed by my family for the past twenty years. I spent the next decade cataloguing all the plants I could find on those eighty acres, many of which were discovered with the help of my psychic skills.

As I grew older I learned to rely on my psychic senses as a guide in my daily life. I spent most of my career in the field of horticulture. Gardens are living works of art, and I loved creating them. I could concentrate all of my favorite plants into a much smaller area than I found while wandering through the meadows and forests of my youth. I worked at two botanic gardens and honed my craft. Eventually I started a business and created award-winning gardens for customers along the Front Range of Colorado. As the business grew larger, my psychic abilities guided me each step of the way to help the business thrive. I realized my spiritual life and my everyday life were fully integrated and could be mutually beneficial.

My entire life has been a rich tapestry of spiritual and everyday experiences. Each new spiritual insight had a parallel in my daily life. Each challenge in my daily life was mirrored by internal doubts or frustrations along my spiritual path. My inner and outer life was simply my life. When I integrated both sides of my life and allowed both aspects of myself to flow together freely, I felt liberated. Both the inner and outer sides to our entire self can feed off and help each other become stronger and wiser. Living an integrated life positively affects the quality of our life and the character strengths we bring to our life.

I believe everyone has the potential in them to become psychic. If people only trusted more in the abilities they're already tapping into, they could transform their lives. The purpose of this book, *The Way of the Psychic Heart*, is to lay out exactly how I learned to work with my own psychic abilities, explain the exercises I used to hone my skills so you can do the same for yourself, and reveal some common roadblocks encountered as we embark on our spiritual paths.

How the Book Is Organized

The Way of the Psychic Heart is an introductory course on psychic development. I believe our psychic abilities come from open hearts, and all the exercises in *The Way of the Psychic Heart* are designed to open your heart as you open to your psychic abilities. I've observed a strong connection between open-heartedness and psychic abilities. The more we connect with our heart, the easier our psychic abilities flow.

I've divided the book into four parts, each of which builds on the one before it. Each part has chapters on a particular topic, and each chapter has special exercises to help you experience the chapter topic for yourself. Feel comfortable with the practices in a particular chapter before moving on to the next one. There is no rush to complete anything. Each person's capacity for learning is different, and each person has natural strengths easily achieved, while others require extra attention. Learning other skills in life, such as playing a musical instrument or a new sport, works the same way. I include recommended practice periods before moving on to the next chapter, but these are just guidelines.

"Part I: Foundation" is the foundational section with two chapters full of several exercises, such as creating sacred spaces, to prepare you for what's to come. Chapter 1, "Getting Started," compares the differences between a heart-centered and a mind-centered path and the importance of starting off the spiritual path on the right foot and living from the heart. You will also learn about the importance of psychic protection. The spirit world, like our everyday world, is a generally safe place, but just as in the real world, there are spiritual areas not always friendly to people and I'll show you how to protect yourself in such situations. Finally, I discuss the topic of memory and spiritual experiences. Many times some of our most poignant spiritual experiences are forgotten. Why? Chapter 1 will tell you.

Chapter 2, "Spiritual Athletes," shows you many ways to maximize the development of your psychic abilities by taking care of your body and conditioning your mind for the challenges ahead.

Now that we have the foundation laid, "Part II: Learning to See with the Three Pillars" explores the practices I used to discover and strengthen my skills. The three pillars of my spiritual life are increasing awareness, developing my intuition, and seeing auras. I call them the Three Pillars and explore them in three chapters: "Developing Awareness," "Seeing Auras," and "Honing Intuition." Each of these abilities helps the next skills develop more easily and completely. For example, if you're trying to see your aura, which is the energy field around your body, but you aren't very aware of your surroundings, your attempts will be more difficult for you than for someone who already has a finely tuned awareness of their surroundings.

Once you've learned to see using the skills in Part II, then you're ready to jump into "Part III: Learning to Listen." There is an invisible world of information surrounding us that has nothing to do with the Internet or satellite transmissions. The information is transmitted energetically amongst every living thing equally. We are born with all the software needed to listen, and most people receive spiritual information whether they realize it or not. The goal of *The Way of the Psychic Heart* is to help you become more aware of your abilities. Three chapters cover several techniques to learn how to better hear what is being transmitted to us from many sources. Chapter 6, "Dreams," covers how to learn from dreams and what different types of dreams mean. Chapter 7, "Automatic Writing," covers automatic writing, an enhanced method of tapping into your psychic abilities to gain access to hitherto hidden information. Chapter 8, "Spirit Guides," covers the topic of spirit guides. I explain what spirit guides are and why they're important for your daily quality of life and happiness.

Many skills can be developed after you've learned to see with the Three Pillars and learned to consciously listen with the techniques in Part III. Before delving in to those advanced skills, it is critical to approach our new spiritual path with the highest integrity and compassion. "Part IV: Being Psychic" explores what it means to live a psychic life and how to integrate your new abilities into your daily life. In chapter 9 you'll learn why to honor the spiritual responsibilities accompanying your new skills. Chapter 10, "Intention," explores the power of intention, a much-discussed and often-misunderstood spiritual concept. Finally, chapter 11 illuminates the joys of joyful living. Having fun and finding your bliss keeps the meaning of life in perspective.

The conclusion, titled "Psychic Is the New Normal," rounds out our exploration of psychic abilities. Everyone is psychic, which is no different from saying someone is athletic or artistic.

Some of us chose to develop other life skills first, whether a job, education, raising a family, or learning to play volleyball, but it's never too late to embrace your naturally occurring and completely normal psychic abilities.

What Is Psychic?

So, what is "psychic"? According to the *Merriam-Webster Dictionary*, *psychic* means "of or relating to the psyche." Well, what's the psyche? According to the same source, *psyche* means "soul or personality." I like the dictionary definition because psychic abilities do actually help us understand the soul and personality of ourselves—people we know and the world around us. In layman's terms, however, being psychic doesn't really mean anything specific. Saying someone is psychic is similar to saying someone is brainy. Both of these terms are very broad, and the word *psychic* encompasses anything extraordinary and extrasensory in the human experience. Some psychics have really good intuition and seem extremely lucky, as if they're always in the right place at the right time. Some can always tell when a person is lying. Both great life skills, wouldn't you say?

But for other people, psychic skills go much deeper and provide truly life-changing experiences. Psychics describe talking to angels and spirit guides, seeing auras, manifesting their deepest desires into reality, even reading people's minds and emotions by empathizing with another person on a very deep level.

Always treat the spiritual path with respect. *You* are the spiritual path; the path lives within you, like your heart or lungs or thoughts. Learning to flex your psychic muscles takes time. Just as you wouldn't walk up to a car and attempt to lift it just because you have muscles, so you shouldn't try any psychic exercise willy-nilly. It takes time to build up your strength and endurance. And even so, some people have certain strengths compared to others and end up having completely different abilities. While some can learn to do everything amazingly well, most folks tend to have a few specialties and are satisfied to focus only on those few skills.

Psychic experiences are common. Many people I've met have told me about at least one amazing experience powerful enough to defy logical explanation. Some are more dramatic than others and many happen randomly, once in a blue moon for no apparent reason. Sometimes people are hesitant to talk about their experiences, but once they start talking, a river of information and emotion pours out of them. Once people know they're being taken seriously, the walls come down and the information comes out.

A friend of mine saw a fairy while jogging in Washington Park in Denver, Colorado, in the middle of the day.

A woman I know suddenly knew beyond the shadow of a doubt that her father and sister were in trouble. They were hiking in eastern Wyoming in the middle of nowhere, and there was no way to reach them. She discovered later that her family had been face to face with an angry bear in the middle of Wyoming's vast wilderness during the time of her premonition.

An acquaintance of mine was driving a truck with her daughter and granddaughter when the truck slid off the road due to icy conditions and landed in a ditch. Within moments she had a flash of another truck hitting theirs. She pleaded with her family to get out of the truck. As soon as they did, the truck she saw in her vision slid off the road and demolished their truck. The women could have been seriously injured by ignoring the psychic premonition.

A rancher I know very well was driving to work one day, but she kept feeling like she had to go back and check on one of the barns. Overnight, winter plunged the area down into subzero temperatures. Though none of her female alpacas was due to give birth anytime soon, she had a feeling one of them was going to. She listened to her intuition and returned home to find a newborn baby alpaca outside in the freezing cold. If she hadn't gone home to check things out, the baby alpaca could have easily died.

I love stories like these, because they reveal a world much more mysterious and connected than we thought possible. And if a large percentage of people I know are having these experiences, no matter how infrequently, who else is? Psychic experiences are not something talked about in our society, but I suspect people would realize how common such experiences are if they were.

I believe everyone does have the capacity to develop their spiritual gifts and become what is called psychic. Becoming psychic is as normal as anything else we are capable of, and it is possible to train anyone in the basic skills needed to open our psychic doors. What happens beyond your natural abilities depends on individual effort, interests, and family history.

This book, *The Way of the Psychic Heart*, contains an introduction to many of the things I've learned over the years. Some of these skills naturally developed as I grew up, while others required serious effort to explore. Learning to become psychic can be a long, slow process.

If you read this book and practice the exercises within diligently, then you, too, can develop your own talents. Whoever is willing to put in the time to practice can have psychic experiences.

Being psychic is normal. We're all born with different natural talents, whether psychic, athletic, intellectual, artistic, or musical. However, all of us can increase any of these skills with dedicated effort and attention. Most things worth doing in life take dedication, and developing the spiritual path is no different. The more effort you make to learn the exercises in the book, the more you'll gain.

As described earlier, I've arranged things in a particular order to help keep you safe as you develop your skills. Chapters flow one to the next in a deliberate manner, and I highly recommend you follow along step by step. Doing so lines things up correctly inside you and prepares the way for your future growth. The mind may be curious to try things from later chapters, but try and be patient. You will have better results with the later exercises if you master the introductory techniques first.

As each new spiritual exercise is explained in this book, surrender with your heart and be open to receive the experience. We may want to hurry up and learn everything quickly with only a little bit of practice, but real gains in life take time and experience to achieve. Some of the things in *The Way of the Psychic Heart* are very difficult to learn and take years of dedication to learn. Often, future techniques won't make sense or be possible until basic abilities have been activated. Again, I don't mean people who have more active psychic abilities are any better or superior to people who don't. Think of the process in terms of sports: an NFL player at the peak of his game is ultimately no better or worse than a high school football coach. They love the sport in equal measure but were born with different natural talents. Either way, their athletic abilities reveal nothing about their personal character. One may be a role model and the other a jerk. It's impossible to judge a person solely on their natural talents.

I have taught both individuals and groups many of these techniques over the past twenty-five years, and I feel strongly that the skills taught in "Part II: Learning to See with the Three Pillars" are very important. Your psychic development will be easier if you master these first before moving on to the advanced skills. Foundational practices help our future skills become stronger and more successful. Those who learned best held the belief that developing psychic abilities was possible. They had open minds and hearts and had no expectation about how their psychic experiences could unfold. Therefore, keep your mind open. Being psychic is possible and is a normal part of our intended life experience. There really is an amazing magic to the world we live in, though; as is often said in fairy tales, "In order to see magic, you have to believe in it."

Some people have a natural affinity for one ability over another, similar to other aspects of human experience. It's rare to find someone who is extremely smart, emotionally compassionate, *and* incredibly athletic. We usually are born with one or another talent, and then have to work on the rest if we want to get good at them. It's the same concept with psychic abilities. Practice makes perfect. In order to be successful with any of the exercises, you have to practice them regularly.

Even with years of practice you may not be able to do everything you want to do all the time. The types of skills you're trying to learn are internal, like concentrating or being a happy person. Other types of learning can be accomplished by simply memorizing facts. The psychic path is much more similar to learning a sport. No matter how hard you try or how perfectly you take care of yourself, you won't always be able to concentrate, and your abilities, whether psychic or athletic, will falter. There will be days when life turns your smile upside down and you feel less connected to your heart, the source of all psychic abilities.

When these circumstances arise, be patient and compassionate with yourself. Many psychic abilities have a life of their own. Suddenly you see something crystal clear with no effort whatsoever; understanding just comes to you. But trying to force such an experience to return may seem impossible no matter how hard you concentrate. The world of psychic experiences does not adhere to the rules of our everyday life we experience in a job. There are many mysteries on the path of psychic development. A lot of the effort you make now will benefit you in the future, while your current aptitude is based on past events in your life.

Being Realistic

So why don't more people have psychic experiences on an everyday basis? The reason could be the cliché of telling our children, "It's just your imagination" or our, at least in America, proclivity for the mind and its fascination with distraction. I've seen kids talk about things only a psychic could understand, and their parents come along and hush them, tease them, or otherwise squelch their opinion. Eventually children learn to shut down their abilities. Some parents' egos are naturally and unconsciously fearful of unseen things on a gut level, and their children sense their parents' fearfulness, too. Children don't want to upset their parents or experience being ridiculed by their parents, and therefore shut down their natural gifts out of respect.

Some of us are lucky enough to have parents who either encouraged us with our experiences or weren't around enough to notice what was happening. By the time I spoke of these things to my parents in my junior year of high school, it was too late to shut my abilities down. I'd already decided being psychic was totally cool, and I wasn't planning on stopping. From that point forward I've met many psychics. They helped me realize I wasn't living in a complete fantasy world and that many people can, and do, *see* like I do.

The mystique of "being psychic" exists because people have associated psychic abilities with a certain sense of holiness or "super-humanity." Such fantasies put unnecessary pressure on those who claim such gifts. I hope this book removes these unrealistic perspectives and shows "being psychic" as just another tool in the vast toolbox of human experience. Because being psychic is a normal expression of being human, just like being good at sports, art, or science. Ability varies from person to person, and can be practiced by anyone and perfected by those who give psychic development enough attention on a regular basis. Being psychic doesn't mean you're a good person or a bad person, better or more advanced than anyone else, or in any way, shape, or form superior to others. Being psychic doesn't mean you have unlocked the secrets of the universe and can wield unlimited power over others. Being psychic means you're an ordinary woman or man with some cool psychic skills. We're all just ordinary people. We are all brothers and sisters.

A common business adage is "What gets attention, gets done," and the saying applies to everything we do. We are manifesters. We have the ability to choose what we want to do and then try to do that thing to the best of our abilities. We aren't born with college degrees; we earn them. We (usually) aren't born millionaires; we have to earn every dollar. It's the same with being psychic; if we want to do well, no matter what skills we were born with, we have to practice regularly for years. If enough attention is placed on learning these skills, then our skills improve. If not, they won't.

All we have to do is practice. Practice because, just as in martial arts, you never improve your skills by thinking about how good you'll be someday. You have to actually go out there and practice as often as you can if you hope to get better and open up to your amazing psychic potential. Most people I've taught to see auras start out seeing them the same way I did: whites and grays first, then colors later on. There are benchmarks along your path to show the progress you are making. Intuition is incredibly fickle and fallible at first; 50/50 or worse results are common due in large part to second-guessing by the mind. The mind will actually talk you out of the right answer time and time again. Slowly, with practice, you learn to separate your thoughts from your feelings and home in on your intuition. Eventually, your intuition integrates into everything you do. But developing intuition takes practice—lots and lots of practice.

This book, *The Way of the Psychic Heart*, provides keys to develop your psychic abilities. Afterward, your development is up to you. Take your psychic development as far as you want. I highly recommend tempering the mind's desire to master everything with the heart's desire to live in balance. None of these skills are requirements for being alive. Similar to becoming more athletic or creative, some psychic skills make life much easier for you, especially developing your intuition. You feel more balanced and present in the world. Others require lots of energy and time to perfect and are affected by lifestyle choices, psychology, and physical health.

I hope you enjoy what you're about to read. Proceed at your own pace, on your own time.

Part I

Foundation

Chapter One
Getting Started

The best and most beautiful things in the world cannot be seen
or even touched—they must be felt with the heart.
—HELEN KELLER

As we start a spiritual path, it is easy to approach the task like
any other task in life. We set out to achieve a goal, and when
we reach it we celebrate. The more effort and care we invest
in developing a skill, the more reward we feel when we see the
results of our efforts.

Being goal-oriented is not to be confused with a competitive
approach. An especially competitive person tries to develop their
abilities (which are seen as "powers") as fast as possible, better
than anyone who has come before them, and then secretly (or
publicly) wishes to be recognized for their achievements. The
ego can become single-minded and extremely focused on an attempt to be the best, leading to unbalance in all areas of our life.

Every ego is focused on achievement, individual expression, power, and recognition. In a gentle, balanced way, the ego is a helpful tool and keeps us interacting with the world at large while maintaining a sense of self. A healthy ego protects us, inspires us to achieve, and helps us appreciate the vast variety the world presents to us. In a negative way, an overdeveloped ego is disinterested in the world and cares only for its own comfort. Instead, the ego considers itself absolutely fine and perfect, and seeks to control the world around it into something compatible with its own lifestyle.

Another common fallacy says the spiritual path is better than the worldly path. In reality there is no difference; everything is important, and spiritual pursuits have gravity to them in the same way physical things do. Two variations are: one, the development of spiritual gifts indicates a person is more advanced than other people; and, two, it's best to pull away from the "real world" to focus on spiritual things like a monk or nun might choose to do.

These approaches prolong, confuse, and stunt the true spiritual path. Spirituality is as natural as, well, Mother Nature herself. Every living thing has a form of spiritual or extrasensory abilities. Our modern culture has little experience with such things and thus deems them "extra"-sensory or "super"-normal. In fact, psychic experiences are normal. And having any skill in life simply means you have a skill. Being psychic is really as normal as any other life skill.

There are many people who can help us along the way. Teachers of all types are available on the spiritual road of self-discovery. No matter from whom you choose to learn, people who have traveled the path longer or farther than you can share their experiences and help you through the rough spots of your spiritual journey. However, teachers are never better than you. A true teacher respects you, and it is appropriate to show them the same respect. A true teacher never demands you honor them and their needs over your own in any way. Learn what you can from a teacher but remember to maintain your own personality, life, friends, and family connections and job. Just as you never sell your soul to become a professional athlete or scientist, you should never give up yourself to follow another's path.

Staying true to yourself in a heart-centered manner leads you down your spiritual road much faster and farther than you could have by following a teacher blindly along the teacher's own path. We are all unique, and it is important to learn to embrace our own way. Keeping your individuality may seem like a delicate balance at times, but with practice you will feel the difference between your path and someone else's.

An athletic coach is recognized for their ability to get athletes to train harder or become better at a particular sport, but we never give all the credit for someone's athletic ability to their coach. The relationship of coach to athlete is a partnership at best, with the major effort put in by the athlete. In the same way, no guru holds the key to your spiritual growth. Teachers have techniques and experience, but it is up to you to actualize these things.

Originally a guru, medicine teacher, or other spiritual guide was a person entrusted to care for you, like a parent to a child. In the Native American tradition, an apprentice was often spiritually adopted by their teacher to show the strong bond between them. Teachers could only care for another student if they could afford to do so. Students often brought gifts, groceries, tobacco, or other things out of pure joyful gratitude, but gifts were never expected, and gifts never meant money. When I hear about how gurus are charging excessive money of their students, or having sex with them, I'm saddened. Such people are preying off the seekers and are not living a heart-centered life. The lure of many followers, wealth, and fame is often too tempting for the ego to resist.

Cultivating such a business model is not what the path is about.

Swami Vivekananda, a Hindu monk, once said, "Each soul is potentially divine. The goal is to manifest this divinity within by controlling nature, externally and within. Do this either by work or worship or psychic control or philosophy—by one or more or all of these—and be free. This is the whole of religion."

Such a perspective does not come from the heart. The mind and ego focus on controlling their inner and outer environments. Such control does not help us open our heart and become loving, conscious people integrated into all the various forms of life surrounding us. *The Way of the Psychic Heart* focuses on the heart. Through surrender and yielding, we learn to remove our walls to natural spiritual growth. One outcome of a heart-focused spiritual path is the natural development of our psychic gifts.

There is no need to withdraw from the world or feel separated from the rest of your life. Practicing a spiritual path in the everyday world allows you to grow much more quickly than in a monastery. Once you are able to *see* with your complete physical and psychic senses, you realize there are many artificial things you do. Growing and maturing on the spiritual path means confronting these aspects of yourself and moving through them.

Becoming a part of a greater whole opens us up to sense many happy and wonderful things in the world. Living holistically opens us to experience others' pain and confusion, often triggering realizations about our own pain and suffering. To grow, we must embrace and move through the negative and positive. Embracing all aspects of life in a loving way puts us in a vulnerable position threatening to our ego. Try to remember we don't have to take negative experiences any more seriously than positive ones. Sometimes we need help working through an issue. Seek out what is needed to grow and move on. Once a lesson is learned, we move to the next learning opportunity in a natural and organic way. There is no need to push and strive on the path of the heart.

Heart before Mind

There are many advantages to developing a heart-centered spiritual path. Life experiences are more intense, and the feeling of being present in every moment grows sweeter as your practice deepens. Surrendering yourself to vulnerability and the uncertainty of living life open to possibilities, of embracing the concept of "I'm not there yet," is very liberating. Vulnerability allows for a more rich and complete experience of love. Love comes in many forms, and each has many unique and beautiful things to teach us.

In my experience, the more loving we are, the more complete our psychic awakening. I've known many people with psychic abilities who are not nice people, and I'm not saying psychic awareness is impossible to achieve with a closed heart. People with closed hearts have a more difficult time achieving the advanced levels of psychic development.

For now just remember the key to a successful spiritual practice is one founded on love. Anything diminishing love eventually becomes an obstacle to your path. Better to deal with these obstacles now while things are fresh and you haven't had time to become set in your ways.

Negative emotional states of being can also feel like obstacles on our path. Approaching what are usually emotionally charged experiences with the mind can be very confusing. The mind is not supposed to be able to deal with such things. The mind is an organ, like the lungs or the liver. So what is the purpose of the mind? The purpose of the mind is to create a safe and solid "experience box" within which we can safely live. The mind's experience box says, "An apple is always a fruit," or "A woman is different from a man." As we grow up, the mind's experience box fills with data and facts. The brain's job is to store and organize information about the world around us. But the center of our consciousness is not centered in our brain.

Once we are self-reliant, fully actualized spiritual beings, we no longer need the mind to protect us. We realize our consciousness derives from the energy body surrounding and pervading our physical body. The brain, like the heart and lungs, is an honored and respected part of our body. Without the brain we could not function. But once we reach a certain point in our spiritual awakening, we can make our own decisions. We flow with life and meet each new experience head on with joyful surrender. Getting from where you are to there is a long, slow process, so be patient.

At first the differences between the heart and the mind appear subtle, but after a while it's easy to tell the difference between them. I grew up overly focused on the mind, and in middle school my imbalance negatively affected my blossoming spiritual awakening.

By the time I reached middle school—seventh and eighth grades—I had been practicing many of the techniques featured in this book. Due to several life circumstances, I wasn't a very heartfelt kid. I was overly intellectual and felt separate from the world around me. My perception that I was alone in the world was probably one of the reasons I never spoke about my psychic experiences. The world was "out there," separate from me, and it seemed like a good idea to use my psychic abilities on "it" and see what happened. I had no respect.

I continued experimenting with other methods of control. I read in a book about something called "cloud busting," wherein you were supposed to stare at a cloud and mentally will it to evaporate. The idea sounds silly now, but at the time cloud busting seemed like a normal thing to do. I was pretty good at it.

My desire to control the weather came to a head when I thought up the idea to summon lightning during thunderstorms. I waited for Michigan's infamous summer thunderstorms to roll in to town and tried calling down lightning with my will. It worked. I continued practicing for several months. One night we were expecting another storm. My bedroom was on the third floor of our house, and I stared out the window at the gathering storm. I began the process of calling down the lightning. But with the mind nothing is ever enough, and so I wanted to do more than just call down lightning far away. I got the mad idea to call lightning down on my street. The lightning struck closer and closer. Zaps of lightning struck closer and closer in a straight line toward my house. Finally, lightning struck a tree behind the neighbor's house across the street.

My vision switched black, then filled with the most ancient, wrinkled old Native American woman's face. *"Stop messing around with things you don't understand!"* she screamed. She was in such a rage, spittle flew from her mouth as she screamed at me. I was so completely shocked and embarrassed by somebody, or some spirit, watching me pull my tricks all over town that I swore I'd never do anything bad like that again. I felt intense anguish. I mean, she was pissed off! I told myself I had no idea there were rules for psychic abilities. Yet my heart had always known. The next morning I walked up the street under the shade of the summer trees and prayed to God to take away all my abilities until I learned to express them from my heart.

I went to bed and practiced seeing my aura swirling around my arm as usual, but I couldn't see anything. After some serious effort I was able to make out the first skinny layer hugging the body and a little of the next layer, but all I saw was white. I was no longer able to see colors.

Because of my sincere request the day before, I had to start learning everything all over again. I had to wait until I was twenty-one for many of my gifts to come back to me. Some never did, but having re-learned my abilities from the heart opened up a whole new world of spiritual experiences and made my earlier experiences pale in comparison. I also experienced the vast differences between following the path of the mind and the path of the heart.

The way of the mind was quick to learn, yielded visible immediate results as I learned to control the world around me, and stroked my ego. There was a quick rush of accomplishment, but then I wanted more. The experience left me hollow inside. The way of the heart has been much more satisfying. Following my heart is a much richer and more satisfying way of living. Life is always full of surprises and without boundaries, truly magical and deeply alive. If you can learn from my experience, please don't take the quick path. Be patient and really try to develop your spiritual gifts from the heart.

So, how will we know if what we're doing is following the heart or the mind? Being able to tell the difference is especially important if we're new to psychic development and spiritual perspectives in general.

One very effective way to instill particular habits or thoughts into our everyday life is through creating and repeating affirmations. Affirmations are single sentences or short phrases embodying something we want to incorporate into our life. Affirmations are typically written down on a piece of paper. I purchased a 3" x 5" mini-notepad especially for my affirmations. The little thing fits in my pocket so I can carry it with me when I feel like I need to stay focused on a particular goal or intention.

The following exercise is very easy and straightforward, which is how all the exercises in this book are designed to be. Each exercise can be repeated for the rest of your life as often as you need. Even with affirmations, the more open-minded you are about the possibility of these exercises actually helping you develop, the more your psychic skills will actually help you improve.

Let's get started.

Exercise:
Affirmations

I believe people always get what they ask for. The problem is people don't usually know what they're asking for. We say all kinds of things, and our desires frequently change from day to day. One way to focus on what we really want and minimize the impact of all the other random things we say is through the practice of repeating affirmations.

Affirmations are thoughts spoken out loud to convey your intentions to the world at large and to your subconscious. Affirmations are best done when you are relaxed and calm. The calmer you are, the deeper the intention travels into your subconscious. The affirmations on the following pages can be repeated a few times a week until you feel their effects showing in your life. Everything we do in life is food for our soul. Doing things repeatedly with no break doesn't give us time to digest the experience, and we spend a lot of energy trying to cope with an overload of experiences. Therefore, there is no need to repeat affirmations all day every day. Taking breaks is an important part of achieving goals in life. Repeating your affirmations three or four times per week is plenty.

Be as present as possible while performing each exercise in order to gain the most from your experiences. One way to be present for an experience is to take a pause between what you were doing before an exercise and the exercise itself. Find a comfortable location in which to practice, a pad of paper, and a pen or pencil, and let's get started.

Below are several affirmations. Read through them and choose those that most resonate with you. All of the following affirmations mean the same thing, but are written differently for different personality types. Copy those that resonate for you into your notebook.

"I live from my heart and serve the Light in all areas of my life."

"I open myself to new abilities as my heart guides me each step of the way."

"I patiently surrender to my psychic learning process."

"I love the way my soul develops and am happy with my magical life. Every day I open to my spiritual abilities with joy."

"I am psychic."

"I promise to use my psychic abilities from my heart, and never disrespect or control another person with these gifts."

"I respect my boundaries and those of others around me. I honor everyone's process and never interfere with anyone's *learning style or speed. I know everyone is given the right lessons to learn for their highest good at the best possible time. As I learn to develop my psychic gifts, I promise not to use my insights into others as a way to influence or force their own personal development."*

Find a comfortable spot in which to practice. Take several deep breaths and relax. Feel your body and what it's standing, sitting, or lying on. Take another deep breath and hold it for a few seconds. Exhale and relax even more deeply. Repeat one or more of the affirmations out loud. Affirmations can be spoken in a whisper or a shout or anything in between; the point is to make a sound your ears can hear. As you repeat these words, really believe the value and strength the words carry. Feel the truth in the words. Take a deep breath and feel or visualize what a person living one of these affirmations is like. Exhale and relax.

Pretty easy so far, right? Set aside time to repeat these affirmations several times each week. The words eventually take hold in you and transform the way you see your world. The words feel more and more true and personal.

Sometimes it's difficult to feel anything at all with so many distractions bombarding us every minute of our waking life. If you are an exceptionally intellectual person, your feelings may be limited to the mental ones: irritation, impatience, high or low self-esteem, or pride. Thoughts disguised as emotions can have a very debilitating effect on our daily life.

True emotions are things like joy, sadness, fear, true anger, and happiness, for example. Emotions are often full-body experiences. Clearing and processing true emotions takes place through living from the heart. Clearing mental emotions happens when we agree to think new thoughts about the world and those we interact with. Affirmations are a great way to change the way we think about our reality and help us believe in a new way of being. There is another way to do something similar for our heart.

The following exercise opens you to the feelings coming from your heart. It is important to get to know yourself emotionally because true psychic ability comes from the heart. Learning to live a heart-centered life can start off as a rocky road if you have unprocessed emotional baggage. Living on Planet Earth is almost guaranteed to help you experience some sort of emotional trauma. Experiencing negativity is a normal part of being human. What we do with these experiences determines how easily our psychic abilities come to us and how far we're willing to travel down our spiritual path.

Many people who learn about their psychic abilities have positive initial experiences. However, as your strength and endurance for spiritual exercising build, you see things about yourself needing a little attention and sprucing up. If you have already learned to become comfortable with handling emotions, you'll be much more prepared for the emotional, heart-opening journey ahead.

The abilities of the heart are truly unlimited and connect us to literally everything else in the universe. The only thing between us and universal wisdom is our own self. As we spiritually mature, we also mature emotionally. We become better able to understand the effects of our actions. Spiritually mature people also see what is necessary in a situation and will take action even if what is required is uncomfortable or difficult in the short term. Living from the heart takes courage.

By contrast, an overdeveloped mind can lead to introversion or a lack of "normal" social skills. Those who build their psychic abilities from the mind may find success, but mental power holds too much charge in the brain and can very often lead to insanity. From my perspective, from the way I *see*, an overly developed mind builds up a type of static charge in the auric field, which separates a person from the natural auric energies found in the natural world. The deep separation such a condition creates can lead to mental instability.

I'm not joking about the mental magicians going crazy, whether male or female. Have you ever read or seen stories about evil characters in folk tales, megalomaniacs willing to destroy all of creation to achieve their goals? Have you ever noticed how the villains come across so comically self-centered? Their selfish natures are almost childlike in their simplicity. Developing the mind alone does not allow humans to become true adults, in a spiritual sense. People who use magic to seek power and control have exclusively developed their mental ego and willpower to the detriment of their heart, body, and soul.

Doing things to keep the heart open and humble keeps you from wandering down the mental path. Do something new you probably won't be good at right away and embrace making a fool of yourself. Participate in the world. Get involved in life. Volunteer. Help children, animals, and the elderly. Dance. Sing. Become an artist. Be real and authentic in the world and take care of your daily responsibilities. All of these things develop the heart and keep your emotions and thoughts in balance. These activities are spiritual "food" that you can use to grow your psychic abilities.

Let's begin the next exercise.

Exercise:
Heart Breath

Find a comfortable spot to meditate, free of potential distraction and disturbance. Relax. Take several deep breaths and become aware of your body. Feel your awareness in your body. Feel your arms, legs, head, and torso. Take several more breaths. Hold each one for several seconds before exhaling.

Be aware of your lungs holding the breath. Feel them become energized as you inhale each time. Feel them within your rib cage. Continue relaxing.

Feel the space between your lungs. As you inhale, let the energy your lungs receive energize your entire chest. Smile and receive the energy. Let the energy of the breath come into your heart. Feel the life and happiness in your heart. Inhale into your heart and hold the breath. Allow all tension to gather as you hold the breath, and allow all tension to leave your body completely each time you exhale.

Continue clearing the heart space for a while, until you feel finished.

Now visualize your heart as a glowing light. The color of the light can be anything, but typically people see pink, vibrant green, gold, or silver. No matter which color resonates for you, allow the mind to see the heart space as glowing and alive. Each inhale now builds the energy of the heart and increases the brightness and clarity of the heart's inner light. Feel how alive you are, feel the joy and happiness at being alive.

Over time other things may come to you while performing the Heart Breath exercise, but for now enjoy being present with your newfound heart connection. As much as you are able, allow yourself to hold a feeling of life and joy within your heart as you open your eyes and continue going about your day or night.

Thank yourself for being present with more of who you really are, no matter how much or little of the energy you felt flow through you. Do you feel more present? Are you more aware of the world around you right now? Do you feel refreshed at all, more energized and at the same time more calm? With time and practice, performing the Heart Breath exercise each day will help you build endurance for the tasks laid out in the following chapters.

You don't need to specifically know in words what your heart is doing, but the more you practice, the stronger your spiritual heart becomes. Your spiritual heart processes the experiences of your day. All your thoughts, feelings, physical sensations, and psychic perceptions and interactions, whether conscious or unconscious, remembered or forgotten, are energetically processed and spiritually digested.

Your attention follows your breath. Breathe quickly, and you flit from thought to thought. Breathe slowly and deeply, and you feel more present and calm. Calm presence keeps you in alignment with your spiritual heart and helps in your decision-making processes during the day. With practice you can learn to breathe the heart breath all the time. Living with the heart breath increases your psychic energy reserve and endurance.

The source of your gifts lies dormant in your heart. Not the fleshy muscle under your rib cage but the spiritual one within. You connect to your heart when you feel. Feelings range from positive love and joy to negative fear and sadness. You become reacquainted with your spiritual heart. Your spiri-

tual heart connects to a much larger version of who you are. Become friends with yourself, love yourself, and believe everything you need is within you right now. Even if you don't think so highly of yourself, keep practicing. Your heart opening occurs as you work through the practices in The Way of the Psychic Heart. *Having an open heart makes opening psychic abilities much easier, and ensures you do not become mired in the wily ways of the ego.*

Play keeps the heart and mind in balance. Play keeps the ego modest because play involves the unexpected, and living unexpectedly makes it difficult for the mind to assume what happens next. Regularly surprising the ego with the unexpected prevents it from taking over and commanding your personality in a given situation. Whenever you can, it's a great idea to take advantage of playtime, no matter how old or young you are. Whether it's carefree sports, doing the chicken dance in public, or any other silly little thing proving how immature and fun you are, just do it! Living a joyful life keeps the heart in good shape and the body and mind working in harmony. The ego learns to lose control in safe ways. We'll discuss joyful living in more depth toward the end of the book. Heart breathing is a gateway to having a more playful and magical life.

Psychic Protection

Each place is the right place—
the place where I now am can be a sacred space.

—RAVI RAVINDRA

Creating Sacred Space

Practice in a safe environment whenever you work toward developing your abilities. Developing our psychic abilities enhances the experience of life by connecting us more deeply to what is happening around us. Trying to get in touch with deeper parts of ourselves while fearing for personal safety, being ridiculed or harassed by others, or being in a distracting environment can hamper progress. Learning to concentrate is an important part of the training process, but basic safety needs to be honored as well. Over time you could be in the middle of a proverbial hurricane and be cool as a cucumber with an inner sense of what you need to do next. Until then, find a safe and relaxing place to practice.

Delineate between practice time and non-practice time. Just as there are practices to open us up to our psychic natures, there are also practices to shut our abilities down and to protect us from harm. Some people have an affinity for one or the other. And just because you have to become more "open" doesn't automatically mean you become "closed" again when you are finished practicing. Many very advanced psychics go through life with their psychic senses wide open, which is exhausting. Just as a weightlifter isn't always flexing, it's important for psychics to let go as well.

There are many paradoxical things about being psychic. One of the most interesting is what you don't *see* has a harder time affecting you than if you *see* it, psychically speaking. The ability to tune things out for our own safety comes in handy down the road. Similar to the ostrich with its head in the sand to avoid disaster, we can protect ourselves by turning off our ability to *see* or *sense* the psychic world. We are powerful beings and can shut out what we don't want around us.

However, once we've opened up, it's easy to go through life wide open, spiritually speaking, like a gigantic fish net, catching everything around us. When we open our energy field to focus on the spiritual world around us, we collect many influences into our aura, even our body. People can have physical reactions to influences, including coming down with the flu. In addition, people can dream about other people's lives and become something other than their authentic self. Learning how to properly perform the psychic-protection exercises described in subsequent chapters prevents such negative experiences from happening.

In high school I had no clue what I was doing. I was experimenting all the time, on people, on animals, on the elements. I went with whatever inspiration bubbled up in me, no matter what time of day or night. No idea was too outlandish. I was so wrapped up in my excitement over my flourishing psychic abilities that I didn't stop and think, let alone feel, whether or not what I did was healthy for myself or others.

I also had no idea how to close myself back down. I never realized I had to! As a result, I was open to outside energy influences most of the time. I remember attending a pow-wow in high school. I arrived late for the celebratory dancing, so I visited all the food and vendor booths instead. I had a little bit of cash and wanted to buy a souvenir. There was an old Native American man selling many things from animal parts: rattles, drums, ceremonial garb, necklaces, and the like. One necklace in particular "called" to me. The old man noticed right away and told me its history as he pulled the object out for me to inspect. He purchased it, he said, from an old Indian man he used to know. The necklace was made of bear's teeth, deer sinew, and beads.

The necklace was thick with energy. The old man was selling the necklace for fifty dollars, a lot of money for me at the time. I was so enthralled with the energy of the piece, I bought it. I felt power in the necklace and wanted it for myself. The man bagged up the necklace and handed it to me. I thanked him and walked away.

As I walked away, I put the necklace on and was excited to visit other booths. The piece fit perfectly without needing to be adjusted. However, within minutes I felt lightheaded and disoriented. Soon I felt so bad I became nauseous. I finally took the necklace off and the nausea left immediately, but I still felt woozy. My neck remained sore for hours afterward. I found some water and splashed my neck and face and began to feel a bit better.

I put the necklace back in the bag and went back to my car. I didn't want to bring the thing home, nor did I want to try and get my money back; I didn't want someone else to buy the necklace in the future. I decided the best thing to do was bury it somewhere no one could find it. I picked a spot, said a few kind words, and gave the necklace a proper burial. By the next morning I felt better.

I could have avoided the situation if I had known about psychic protection. I definitely avoid similar items today. Psychics are generally empaths as well, and tune in to things going on in the world hidden from ordinary perception. An empath is a person who is extremely sensitive to the emotions and feelings of others, to unseen energies or "vibes" surrounding people, objects, or situations and places. Empaths tune in to other people in ways ordinary people do not. Native American culture is still alive with magic and mystery, despite what people say about such things fading away in the days before Europeans showed up. The necklace had an energy field strong enough to glow like a bright light to me. Being inexperienced, I couldn't resist its thrall.

Years later I read a similar story about Carlos Castaneda, the metaphysical writer who wrote extensively about unconventional shamanic experiences. He relates a story about how he saw a shiny object off in the distance in the deserts of Mexico.

He walked over to the spot and saw a small, carved object poking out of the earth. He picked it up and made a necklace out of it. Within hours he began acting erratically and getting into trouble until a kind stranger advised him to get rid of the necklace forever. He, too, buried the thing and felt better. The parallels were remarkable.

Altered States

Speaking of Carlos Castaneda—who was known for his use of hallucinogenic plants to induce spiritual experiences—reminds me to mention something about altered states of consciousness.

In a nutshell, hallucinogenic substances, even marijuana, are hindrances on the type of spiritual path described in *The Way of the Psychic Heart*. A heart-centered path does not require the use of mind-altering substances to be successful. In native cultures, a shaman, healer, or medicine person spiritually partners with special plants and mushrooms as part of their spiritual path. Sometimes these are used to help bring their apprentices, or students, to another world. Not everyone is given these substances, and those who are only experience them under the direct supervision and guidance of their teacher. The entire process is considered holy and special and is not undertaken lightly. The plants and mushrooms involved are considered living, sentient beings who need to be met and partnered with before experiencing their effects in the body.

I'm writing about a different way of doing things. I'm writing about a heart-centered path that seeks to increase clarity, awareness, and attention in all areas of life at all times. Using external objects as a crutch or starting point is unnecessary, whether the objects be plants, magic wands, crystals, or Tarot cards. All of these objects are external to you. On a heart-centered path, you're dealing with the real you. You're important. You matter. You have immense value. You were also born with everything you need to begin your journey. Drugs and other substances that change your consciousness are ultimately hindrances on a heart-centered spiritual path.

Never practice while drunk. *Never* practice while high. In fact, never practice psychic development while under the influence of *any* drug that alters your mood, mind, or body, or "expands your consciousness," whether prescribed by a doctor or sourced illegally. Illegal drugs, especially hallucinogens, appeal to people for many reasons but don't allow you to have an authentic experience of your own. Instead, you merely watch the effects of the drugs on your psyche. Wouldn't you rather have your own unique experience without the crutch of an external substance? Humans are born with everything needed to develop their psychic abilities; nothing external is required.

On the spiritual path, things start small and build up slowly over time to a never-ending crescendo dwarfing drug-induced experience by comparison.

Some people have defended the use of hallucinogenic drugs to me by explaining that Native Americans, Siberian shamans, African Voodoo cults, and other traditional groups of people use such substances in their ceremonies. The same logic also manifested in some college acquaintances who told me that since Jesus drank wine at the Last Supper, there was nothing wrong in getting wasted at a party, spiritually speaking. Obviously sipping wine during a sacred meal is not the same as getting wasted at a party; the same concept applies to hallucinogens. Most of these "sacred ingestions" people have told me about happened on camping trips in the woods with a group of people who decided to get high after having a few drinks. Under such circumstances, the sacred aspect is lost. Casual drug use is a hindrance to clear psychic development.

Many illegal substances are addictive as well. Some create mental addictions, as with marijuana, while others are physical. Over time the amount of a substance required to generate hallucinogenic experiences increases. Many of these hallucinogens are actually poisonous to the body, as with *Amanita muscaria*, or fly agaric mushroom, and long-term use damages the body.

Those are the more mundane reasons to avoid drugs, but from a psychic's point of view, there are other reasons as well. The auras of people who regularly do drugs are thick and smoky compared to non-users' auras, which are more liquid and shimmery. Everything alive has an aura and a consciousness, including plants. Hallucinogenic plants have very strong, bold spirits.

Plants of all types are alive and truly aware. Long-term ingestion of hallucinogenic substances creates a spiritually dependent condition in drug users. The spirits of the ingested psychotropic plants combine in the drug user's energy field. The resulting auric mishmash does not look healthy.

A final reason not to take drugs is almost mechanical. Drugs force open the doors of higher perception. Forcing doors of perception open artificially has been known to break these doors permanently. In my view, having your psychic doors forced open is why some people who take drugs only once go insane, while others can appear to handle their use for many years. Different people are born with different strengths and weaknesses, and some are born with weak spiritual doors. Once an experience shatters the door, people can quite literally become unhinged.

In high school I met a woman with a remarkable story. One day she opened up to me about her psychic experiences and her family history. Her family came from a long line of Polish gypsies. While her grandmother was fully initiated in the tradition, her mother wanted nothing to do with it and refused to teach the woman anything at all. However, over the years the woman went around her mother and learned a few ceremonies from her grandmother. One ceremony was the final ceremony traditionally performed in order to become a full-fledged medicine woman. Once a woman performed the ceremony, she completely came in to her psychic abilities.

Well, long before I met her, when the woman telling me her story was young and reckless, she partied a lot and did lots of drugs. One night after getting plastered and flying high on drugs, the woman decided to perform the final ceremony following her grandmother's instructions. Usually what she was about to do only happened after years of training.

The ceremony was very complicated. Two other people had to be present, one of whom was not associated with the tradition at all. The final act required her to mildly slit her wrists to symbolize dying to her old way of being. As she recounted her tale, she pulled up her sleeves and showed me the scars on her arms. She didn't feel any different after the ceremony was over so she went home and slept.

The next morning she awoke to the sounds of a noisy argument taking place outside her window. She also had a hangover. She was not in the mood for early-morning noise and jumped out of bed to yell out the window at her neighbors. She was shocked when there were no people outside to yell at. She followed the sound of the voices up into a nearby tree, where several squirrels were engaged in a heated conversation. Needless to say, she was shocked beyond belief. Fascinated, she got dressed and went outside. She heard a combination of human and animal thoughts. At first she was excited, but she soon realized she couldn't stop hearing the voices. No matter where she went, she heard voices. For *years* afterward she had no control over her ability, and the constant barrage of voices nearly drove her mad.

I met her fifteen years after she performed the ceremony. When I met her she had learned to control the voices and could choose when to tune in and when to tune out. She said she tuned things out most of the time.

As a side note, she attended a Polish festival one summer at a local Polish Catholic church in Grand Rapids. While exploring the various booths at the event, a nun walked up to her and said, "Aren't you a little young to be a healer?" The woman was dumbfounded. She asked the nun how she knew, and the nun pointed to the particular location and shape of the scars on her arms. The woman asked the nun questions, but the nun had nothing else to say.

I share the woman's story as a warning to those who are tempted to engage in magical practices under the influence of drugs with no thought of the outcome. What was done on a whim caused my friend years of anguish as she tried to get control of the voices in her head. When I knew her, she was also sad because she had a foot in two worlds with no one to help guide her forward or back.

Along with avoiding drug use, another rule is never to practice while unprotected around negative energy or people. People surrounded with negative energy project their negative energy into their surroundings. Unshielded, a newly psychic person can absorb negative energy from being so open. In addition, certain negative people, areas, or situations unconsciously "feed" off other people's reactions to their negative state. Avoid these types of people until you've learned to seal up and protect your energy field from prying eyes. Or at least avoid practicing around them.

Let's practice owning our space, the first step on the path to learning psychic protection. The practice is designed to be simple yet effective.

Exercise:
Owning Your Space by Smudging

An easy and very old method to create sacred space is to burn some incense and verbally state your intentions in whatever space you intend to practice. The exercise is simple and goes as follows:

First, purchase a bundle of white sage and a braid of sweetgrass. Buy separate bundles if you can. Sage and sweetgrass are often sold wrapped together in one bundle, but having them separate is preferred. You'll see why in a few minutes.

Traditionally, white sage smells "bad" to negative energy, and its smoke is therefore used to clear away bad vibes from a room, a house, your body, or any other object. Sweetgrass smells "sweet" to positive, helpful spirits and draws them in to a space as a blessing. Both are typically available at herb shops or New Age bookstores. Even health food stores carry them.

We will start by blessing a room, but the technique can be modified to bless any size space indoors or outdoors. Light the sage bundle, then blow out the flame so only glowing embers remain. A thick, white, gentle smoke rises from the bundle. Now use the smoking bundle like a pencil to define every edge of the room, including windows, doors, and other openings. Use the smoke emanating from the bundle as a wash to bless the space.

Smoking a house, your body, or any object is called smudging. Smudge the frames of the room: bottom, corners, both sides and top. Smudge any nooks and crannies to remove any old, stagnant, or negative energy, too. As you smudge, state aloud the following words: "This is **MY** house. This is **MY** space. I am here, in my world, in my space, for my highest good. Anything against my well-being is no longer invited into this space and must leave **NOW**. Any high vibrational beings of light and love can stay to assist in my growth and well-being."

Repeat the words as many times as you need to in order to really feel the truth and power of your words. If at any time the bundle stops smoking, simply relight it as before and then blow out the flame.

When the smoke fades, I gently blow on the smoke, like fanning the embers of a dying fire, and the smoke increases. I don't recommend fanning a smoldering object unless you feel very comfortable working with what is basically a burning object in your hands.

When you've finished, rinse the sage briefly in water to stop the smoking.

Let your awareness tune in to the room now. Does the room feel different in a positive way, such as lighter or clearer? We're halfway done. After the negative vibes have been sent away, it's time to bring in the good ones.

The next step is to do the same smudging technique with the sweetgrass braid. Sweetgrass braids are usually tied more loosely than the sage bundles. Therefore the braid may go out several times as you smudge. Simply relight as needed until you are finished. Repeat the same process of defining your space with the smoke, including windows, doors, or other openings in the home, and repeat the following words: "Hello, spirit guides, angels, and archangels, any of my loving spirit friends, and all higher vibrational beings. Please come into my home to bless, heal, and protect it from harm. Bless me and all who stay here with me. This is my home and my space, and I want only the highest vibrational blessed Light to fill my home. Thank you."

Depending on your religious perspective and affinities, change the wording of whom or what you want to invite into your house. Invoke God, Allah, your ancestors, Mary, or any other positive, uplifting personification of love and light.

Whatever you choose to say, repeat the words as often as needed until you really feel the power and intention in what *you are asking for. Lower vibrational energies often enter a home because the space is empty. Nature hates a vacuum, and the concept applies to spiritual empty spaces, too. But as you mature along your spiritual path and become a more conscious spiritual being, your intentions hold more weight and carry more conviction. When you bless your personal space, you get to choose what lives in your space. We are co-creative manifesters on Earth, and our words are laced with magic, whether we know it or not.*

Repeat the blessing process as often as you'd like. Be aware of changes occurring in your house each time you smudge. Done correctly, your personal space becomes lighter and happier.

Exercise:
Heart Smudging

Once the smudging is complete, you are ready to move on to a more personal step. Smudge whatever space you are in with love from your spiritual heart. Humans have so much more potential than we allow ourselves to remember. Our hearts are extremely magical. The power of love can work miracles. Find a comfortable place to sit and meditate in the space you want to bless. Again, the space may be inside or outside, a single room or an entire building.

Sit comfortably and close your eyes. How you sit doesn't matter—simply be comfortable. Take a few breaths and relax. Become aware of your body and where you are in the room. Become aware of your lungs inhaling and exhaling. Breathe in and out. Relax. Now become aware of the space between your lungs, your heart. Allow yourself to breathe in to your heart. Feel your heart fill with light-filled air as you inhale. Smile as you exhale. Feel the warm happiness inside you grow. Keep breathing for a while, and each time you exhale, feel a warm, happy love fill the room you're sitting in. The light you're creating with your breath fills the space as a very powerful blessing.

The skin around your chest, lungs, heart muscle, or back can feel raw after just a short period of time spent breathing. A raw feeling is normal; your body isn't used to feeling so much energy at one time. Simply stop and breathe normally. Smile, stand up, and move around to dispel the energy you've just concentrated around your spiritual heart center. With time, your endurance grows and you can spend hours heart breathing and feel blissful the entire time.

If you don't feel raw, continue practicing until you are finished with the exercise or become tired. Bring your attention back to your body and open your eyes. Feel the happiness you brought into the world, inside your sacred space, and say aloud, "I bless this space with my healing breath. May my *light protect me all the days of my life and bring joy to those who know me."*

Over time I recommend blessing each room of your house individually. Find comfortable places to practice in each room. Yes, even the bathroom, garage, or other atypical location. Done from the heart, smudging can transform an old stuffy home into a place of beauty and tranquility.

I suggest you perform these exercises at different times of the day and night in order to bless all of the different energies flowing through your house. Despite the modern constructions humans have brought into the world, which disrupt the natural travel patterns of animals and, more slowly, plants, there are other things unaffected by our works.

Have you ever seen deer trails meandering through the forest? Or the winter patterns mice and voles leave in the grass seen after spring's snowmelt? Well, spirits also leave trails, and their patterns of movement can be felt and seen by psychic people sensitive to such things. Different spirits most likely move through your house at different times of the day and night. Some might be kin with the four-legged animals. Others dance through your neighborhood to the patterns of the clouds and winds. Others rise and fall with the ever-changing pulsing of the energy lines of the earth traveling from deep underground up to the surface.

Practicing the heart smudge at different times of day and night in different parts of the house allows all of the different spirits traveling through your local area and home to know you exist. Spirits who *see* you grow in spiritual strength, and respect your personal space. Spirits are required to respect your space and honor your intentions. You're not shown respect out of deference or fear or inferiority to your growing power. All of the spiritual beings I've encountered are just naturally respectful beings—and as exuberant or heavy as their spirits may be—always respect my privacy and personal space.

All aspects of your personal space will hear your intention to bring healing and helpful energies into your life and respond accordingly.

Recalling Spiritual Events

Before we get into the actual practices of *seeing* things psychically, I want to mention something. As I mentioned earlier, there are many paradoxes on the spiritual path. One of the oddest of these paradoxes is when something ridiculously amazing happens—I mean something really big and life-changing—and by the next day you've completely forgotten what happened.

How could someone forget about having seen a ghost, their aura, or a prophetic dream? These are pretty incredible experiences, right? Well, memory loss is unfortunately a common occurrence, and the best way to jog your memory is to write things down in your journal immediately.

But why do we forget? There is one simple reason: our mind is playing tricks on us.

Psychic experiences directly challenge the mind's experience box, the part of the brain telling us what is and what is not real. Some psychic experiences are so "out there" and seem altogether "unreal" that the brain basically says, "Yep. You're right. Nothing weird just happened, so I'll just put the experience in deep storage for you, *mmm-kay*?" The brain presses the reset button on the memory banks of our life experiences and conveniently washes away anything perceived as too unusual.

Who knows? Maybe you've already had amazing psychic experiences and you've forgotten about them! As with many of my life interests, my interest in psychic development goes in fits and spurts and ebbs and flows based on what else is going on in my life. When I first launched my landscape business in 2003, I had no idea how much of a time-suck running a business could be. I had a full-time day job and spent all of my time after work and weekends growing my business. My free time for fun things like finding spirit-filled Nature trails in the wilderness became very limited.

After several years, the business became more stable, and I had more time available for non-work activities. I began meditating again and doing yoga, and after a year or so I suddenly began remembering all of these cool experiences I'd had before launching my business. The busy distractions of the last few years had taught my mind to focus on and remember only work-related or "normal" experiences. Engaging in spiritual activities again retrained my mind to include everything I'd forgotten about in the ensuing years. I was shocked because some of those experiences, at the time, had a major influence on the course of my life. And yet it was as if the experience never happened.

To ensure I didn't forget them again, I wrote everything down for safekeeping. Keep a journal handy at all times. You never know when you need to write something down or when you'll need to jog your fickle memory.

A number of years back, my dad and I went to Beaver Island in northern Lake Michigan. Many magical things live on the islands making up the Beaver Island archipelago, and my dad wanted to see if he could see something there, too. He'd recently retired and found himself with a lot more free time. He'd heard some of my Beaver Island stories and was curious if he could see things there, too. He's by nature a very intellectual person and for the first few days nothing happened. His mind prevented him from seeing all of the magic around him and kept him tuned to the ordinary frequency of the modern world.

He finally had a breakthrough on the shores of Fox Lake on the afternoon of the third day. He allowed himself to let go and lose control. The next day we went out into the woods toward French Bay, down an old gravel road I used to travel on as a teenager but which by then had been abandoned. We turned onto the road and immediately came across a large fallen tree blocking the road. We parked and headed out on foot.

We were the only ones there. There were no footprints in the wet earth of the road; there were no voices, no houses, and no people. Being so isolated from civilization was great. There were lots of Nature spirits doing their thing as we walked by. I saw tree spirits dancing around forgotten glades, fairies zipping through the air above a pond full of water lilies like a horde of dragonflies, earth spirits murmuring in low tones to each other from stone to stone.

The grass-covered gravel road narrowed and banked to our left, and we began the short descent to the bay. We went from walking side by side to single file as the road narrowed to a mere footpath and my dad led the way. Up ahead was an old oak tree. I felt the tree watching us approach so I sent a "Hello" feeling to it from my heart-thoughts. I felt the tree smile back. I told him I was bringing my dad to the island for the first time and I was excited to show him the world of spirits. The tree laughed a low, full, booming laugh.

"Did you hear that?" my dad asked as he whipped around to face me. His shocked face was on full alert. "The tree just laughed!"

Now we were getting somewhere! I explained what happened, and he was extremely excited. We kept walking.

A short while later we were in a deep, young forest of hemlock and juniper, very close to the beach. I psychically heard and saw a group of fairies running along near the tops of the trees singing in their unique song, a combination of chimes and bells and humanlike song. Again my dad stopped.

"Did you hear those voices?"

"No, I didn't hear any voices."

"It sounded like girls giggling off in the woods over there." He pointed toward the spot where I was listening to the fairies singing. He heard their chiming song as girls' laughter.

He was genuinely concerned. "Should we try to find them? There's nothing out here. Do you think they're lost?" He was genuinely concerned a group of children might be lost playing in the woods, laughing without a care in the world.

I asked him exactly where he heard the noise. He thought for a moment and pointed up into the trees. "I guess it came from up there," he said.

"How likely is it a group of kids could climb up there and walk along with us, laughing through the treetops?"

He smiled. "I guess not."

I explained what I saw/heard/felt, and he calmed down. We kept walking. He heard the laughter again as we walked. By then we were close enough to shore to hear the waves crashing on the beach, but the undergrowth was so thick we couldn't see anything.

Suddenly the trail ended and we burst through the forest onto the beach. The road had long since evaporated into a trail, and the beach was completely untouched. We felt that we'd stepped back in time onto a completely unspoiled beach. The rocky beach was alive with pockets of vegetation, insects, and birds. No development within view—just forest, beach, and sea. It took our breath away.

My dad pointed off to our left. "Chad, look!" he said.

Right where the fairies had been laughing through the forest, a small herd of deer emerged onto the beach and hopped away from us, hugging the tree line. In a few moments the herd disappeared back into the forest.

The whole experience had a profound effect on my dad. He experienced firsthand many of the things I talked about. I believe the fairies were playing with the deer as the herd walked through the woods, singing-laughing-talking as they went. In my experience, deer and the fairy folk are good friends and can often be found together.

Fast-forward six weeks. I was back in Colorado, and my dad was in Virginia. We caught up on the phone, and I asked him again how he liked our recent trip. He said he loved the trip, but he made no mention of any of the amazing things we'd experienced. When I asked him specifically about our walk through the woods toward the bay, he said it was cool to see the deer at the beach, and he laughed about how he thought there were kids in the woods.

I asked him about the old oak tree. He had no memory of its laughter. Then I asked him about the fairies in the trees. "What fairies?" he said.

For the next twenty minutes I described our day to him, shared our joint experiences, and tried everything I could to jog his memory. Finally he remembered, and he was amazed he could have forgotten something so profound.

Well, after our phone call I thought my dad would remember what happened on Beaver Island for sure. Maybe a year later the subject came up again, and to my utter amazement he had forgotten *again* about what happened. I was amazed! He remembered many other shared experiences, but none of them had to do with what actually occurred during our walk. Again, I was able to jog his memory and again he couldn't believe he'd forgotten.

Moving ahead seven *years*, it happened *again*. And again I helped jog his memory. Apparently the third time was the charm, as he appears to remember everything whenever I bring it up now. However, now he doesn't believe he'd ever *forgotten*. The workings of the mind are truly amazing. It's a powerful organ of the body and can be both a help and a hindrance on the spiritual path. Regular practice helps the mind accept psychic experiences as being real enough to fit inside its experience box.

I've often wondered how many things happen to all of us every single day that we simply don't remember or subconsciously block out. And not the things like forgetting to pick up the dry cleaning or forgetting to return a phone call. I mean deep, important, potentially life-altering experiences.

There's a strong connection between awareness and memory. When something isn't part of our awareness any longer, we can easily forget about it. For example, how many of us remember all of those mathematical formulas we memorized in high school, or high school French or Spanish? The same principle applies to our spiritual experiences.

When I focus on my spiritual development, I remember my experiences because my consciousness is accustomed to paying attention when psychic experiences happen. During these times I feel more love and happiness within as well. Love energy increases consciousness and understanding, and deepens desire, commitment, and our ability to surrender to the higher calling of our spiritual path. The more attuned I have been to love and loving surrender inside myself, the more I remember all the spiritual things I've experienced. And the times I've chosen to be "normal" and be more active in the modern world of parties, work, entertainment, and duty, I have forgotten those same experiences.

Exercise:
Recording Your Experience

To ensure nothing is forgotten along your journey of spiritual awakening, write down your experiences right away. Don't wait until later; do it now. If something happens, write it down.

Find a special journal in which to record your experiences. It could be special because of its cover style, its shape or size, the number of pages it has, or the options available on each page. For example, I chose a journal with pages lined on one side and blank on the other. A journal with mixed pages allows me to write about an experience and make a little sketch about it if I need to.

Label your journal as being only for recording psychic experiences. Keep a separate journal for, well, journaling or venting. Having a special book makes it easier to locate your special psychic experiences later on. You won't have to rifle through other types of journal entries to find what you're looking for.

As you enter your experiences, leave room at the end for additional notes or future insights. It is very common to find patterns to your experiences. Make notes after certain experiences to help you link them up with previous experiences. For example, when you start working with your spirit guides, covered in a later chapter, if a certain group resonates with you. It's handy to reference their notes and feedback over time.

Many experiences occur in the dreamtime, so I also recommend leaving your journal by your bed at night. If you have a particularly meaningful dream, it's helpful to write it down immediately.

And always make sure you have a pen or pencil available to write with. There's nothing worse than scrambling to find something to write with in the middle of the night, only to forget what it was you wanted to write out with pen finally in hand.

Write your experiences down as soon as you can so you remember the details correctly, all the messages you received, and new friends you've met along the way. Allow yourself to stay open to new experiences. Tell yourself these experiences are a part of your everyday reality.

Chapter Two
Spiritual Athletes

To keep the body in good health is a duty …
otherwise we shall not be able to keep our mind strong and clear.
—THE BUDDHA

There are so many easy parallels between the spiritual and material worlds, because in fact they are the same thing. Everything is spiritual and everything is material. Matter is matter, whether fine or dense. All matter is made of energy, and we are all equally affected by energy depending on its type and strength. Different substances vibrate at different speeds and have different frequencies. Even our cells vibrate at specific frequencies and are mostly empty space, just like the vast cosmos we see in the starry night sky. I believe spiritual substances—whether our aura, a spirit of the forest, or a sudden knowingness about someone—occur because of connections between hitherto undiscovered frequencies of energy.

In other words, psychic energy is a natural phenomenon. Becoming a good psychic is therefore no different from becoming a good basketball player. Both deal with physical things around us, though spiritual things exist beyond the range of our typical, everyday sensory awareness. Or at least that's what our minds have taught us to believe.

So how can we condition ourselves to learn to work with and develop our psychic natures? Shaquille O'Neal says, "Excellence is not a singular habit. You are what you repeatedly do." I love this quote because it can be applied to any endeavor we undertake in life. Whether for sports, business, education, or spiritual development, training is essential. Repetition is essential.

Many athletic and business truisms apply to the spiritual path. Phrases such as "What gets attention, gets done," "Think Win-Win," and "Seek first to understand, then to be understood" from Stephen Covey's book *The 7 Habits of Highly Effective People* are business perspectives completely compatible with your spiritual path.

In the world of business, it is said leaders are not born, they are made. People work hard to become successful. It is the same on the spiritual path, for artists, and for athletes. The most successful people on the spiritual path are those who apply themselves to growing. Practice is an important part of developing your spiritual gifts, as is consistency.

Since the spiritual and material are different aspects of the same thing, in order to get the most out of your practice, take care of your body, mind, emotions, and daily life in equal measure. Caring for your entire being gives you the most energy possible as you practice opening your spiritual gifts.

Just as with any other skill in life, some people are born with an aptitude for one or more life skills, including psychic ability. But for the *vast majority* of humanity, only sustained effort yields significant results.

I hear people joke about some psychic or another who was surprised by some unforeseen event. Unfortunately, this is a common perception about what a psychic truly is. Expecting powers of omniscience from a mere human with psychic abilities is like expecting Shaquille O'Neal to complete the twelve Labors of Hercules simply because he is athletic. Although I'm sure Shaq would give Hercules a run for his money, no one expects him to be godlike in his abilities simply because he calls himself an athlete. Psychics have many different skills and talents at various levels of perfection. The goal of a spiritual athlete is similar to that of a traditional athlete: to improve their skill set.

I spent many years practicing kung fu and many years training in the gym. In both circumstances, my Sifu (kung fu teacher) and my personal trainer told me I am only competing against myself. My training was a way to learn more about myself and become healthier and stronger. Increased self-awareness and strength is what we can expect from our spiritual workouts as well.

The healthier you are, the more effective your spiritual practice. I realize there are many chain-smoking, alcoholic, or otherwise unhealthy psychics. Many of them are amazingly gifted. So I'm not saying it's impossible to find an unhealthy psychic; I'm just saying if you take care of yourself, you'll add an even greater depth to your practice. Excess food waste in the body, whether stored as fat or simply flowing in your bloodstream or lymphatic system, negatively affects your clarity and inner strength and endurance. From my perspective, body toxins negatively affect your ability to *see* with your psychic senses. We can only see at our level of development and below. Why lose your edge and limit your ability to see due to something completely within your power to change and improve?

In a way, taking care of the body honors your presence here on Earth and shows gratitude for the gift of life. In the Bible there is a message about the sacredness of the body. It's found in 1 Corinthians 6:19–20: "Do you not know that your body is a temple of the Holy Spirit? Therefore honor God with your body." Take care of your body; eat right, drink plenty of water, exercise. Take care of your life; leave the world better than you found it, help people, be kind. These things give you clarity, and clarity is what you need to have sharp, reliable psychic senses.

Seeking clarity isn't rocket science, but finding clarity can be difficult. Achieving a sense of clarity in life takes a lifetime of effort—a lifetime of surrendering your mind in honor of your intuition—before you feel a clear connection between you and your higher self, but it can be done. You can become a spiritual athlete. Keep the long game in mind. With a long-term perspective we have the patience to build endurance and slowly make skill improvements over time.

Then again, you may not want to take your practice to such an extreme level. The choice is yours. Your spiritual awakening and psychic development are supposed to be fun and help bring more joy into your life. As with all practices, it's up to you to find your comfort level and set your own goals.

The Good Householder

On the spiritual path it is important to care for all aspects of your life. The concept of the Good Householder holds wisdom for those on a spiritual path. The Good Householder is probably most widely known to people from the Far East, but a wide variety of cultures and religions have mentioned similar concepts. I first heard of the Good Householder while studying the works of Georges Ivanovich Gurdjieff, an amazing spiritual seeker and teacher active from roughly 1880 to 1949. So, what is a Good Householder?

A Good Householder is someone who takes care of their mortal affairs. In addition to taking care of the body, a Good Householder earns enough money to support their life. On the spiritual path a Good Householder is someone who develops a strong earthly foundation and handles their life responsibilities head on. For a Good Householder who is also a spiritual teacher, it means a teacher who takes care of their students as members of their very own family. A teacher only had as many students as they could support while handling their other life duties.

Perhaps not all aspects of the Good Householder are embraced by our modern culture, but the key concept will, I hope, inspire you to take care of your daily responsibilities and leave the world in a better place than you found it. It does no good to shirk daily life to live a spiritual life somewhere as a monk or nun. Instead, embrace daily life and learn to perfect your spiritual ways while in the midst of all of life's beauty and charm, chaos, and stress.

No matter where you are on the spiritual path, taking care of your body and life provides a good balance to your spiritual practice, and keeps you grounded in the "real world." Embracing life responsibilities shows a sensibility compatible with spiritual training. Being responsible and grounded shows you are able to handle stress and discern what is important for your well-being. People seeking spirituality as an escape from the world are subject to self-deception along the spiritual path as well.

Another common saying is "No matter where you go, there you are." This means our world does not need to be transcended or changed; heaven is here on Earth right now. Magic and enlightenment are all around us. All we must do is change our own perception to be able to see heaven on Earth. We can choose to see positivity all around us and live a positive life. Learning the skills of the Good Householder forms a solid foundation on which to grow your spiritual practice.

Skills of a Spiritual Athlete

How do we know if we are being a spiritual athlete?

Let's start with the body. Think of it as a battery with a certain charge. Different things in life add to the charge, while other things take it away. On the spiritual path some things require more of your battery's charge than others.

Different body types and personality types have different tolerances for certain things and different levels of maximum energy. These are general guidelines beneficial to everyone. What follows is a brief quiz to help you assess where you're at as a spiritual athlete. It takes into account physical, mental, emotional, and daily-life criteria to come up with a score.

Exercise:
Spiritual Athlete Self-Reflection

The next exercise is a series of questions designed to show you where you're at physically, mentally, and emotionally. Re-evaluate your answers every quarter or year to recognize your progress. I also recommend getting a physical exam by a doctor or a nutritionist to help you engage in healthier eating and lifestyle habits.

Physical Health Quiz:

- Do you exercise three or more times per week, whether at the gym or through sports or outdoor activities? If not, are you open to exercising, even simply going for regular walks?

- Do you stretch three or more times per week through yoga, Pilates, or a similar structured program? Staying flexible is an important part of a healthy lifestyle. Consult your doctor to see if a more active lifestyle is right for you.

- Do you eat the recommended daily servings of fruits and vegetables? If not, strive to incorporate more of these healthful foods into your diet.

- Do you have low cholesterol? If not, consult your doctor or a nutritionist about ways to lower it. Generally speaking, high cholesterol is indicative of an unhealthy lifestyle, and being physically unhealthy can impede your progress as you continue down your spiritual path.

- Do you have a sedentary job? If so, what activities do you enjoy doing to provide more movement or exercise for the body?

- Do you eat organic foods whenever possible? If not, begin doing so. There are many benefits to eating organic foods. Ask a nutritionist for more information.

- Do you eat a balance of protein and other foods? Excess protein has been shown to be a factor in several health conditions. Consult your doctor or nutritionist for more information about the health benefits of a balanced diet.

Mental Health Self-Assessment:

- Are you able to meet the responsibilities in your life? What is the biggest distraction to accomplishing your daily tasks? Is there anything you can do?
- Are you a curious person? Do you enjoy learning, engaging in new activities, or otherwise expanding your life experiences?
- Do you meditate? If so, how does meditation affect your mental state? What is your favorite way to meditate? Are you able to completely stop your mental chatter?
- Are you confident? If not, what are some areas where you experience self-doubt or anxiety? What are some things you can do to become a more confident person?
- Are you kind to others? If not, what triggers you to believe being unkind is okay? Under what circumstances do you feel others deserve to receive your negativity?

Emotional Health Checklist:

- Are you easily affected by the actions of other people? What affects you the most?

- Do you take time for yourself each week? What do you do?

- Are you patient with others, especially under stressful circumstances? If not, what triggers feeling impatient?

- Are you fluid with your emotions? Fluid with both positive and negative emotions or just one? What are some ways to become a positive emotional person?

- In stressful situations, are you able to keep your cool? Are you able to de-stress whenever you wish? How?

- Do you find joy in life through hobbies, sports, or other creative outlets?

- Is your life full of as much love as you want?

Daily Life Quiz:

- Do you find joy in your job? Do you find joy in your relationships with others? If not, is feeling more joyful important to you? Why or why not?

- Are you able to support your lifestyle through your chosen profession? If not, what are you willing to do in order to change these circumstances?

- Are you able to fulfill your daily responsibilities? If not, what are some key distractions for you?
- Do you consider yourself a helpful person? How could you become even more so?

Use these questions as a way to self-assess your progress toward becoming a Good Householder. The more you can answer yes than no, the more you're on the right track. The more you embody traits of the Good Householder, the more endurance you'll have and the more energy you'll have to become a spiritual athlete.

The body is the temple of the spirit. Take care of the body, and you will have an easier time developing your psychic abilities. Healthy living means more energy for your spiritual batteries and more fun experiences with your blossoming psychic skills. Honor your body as an ally on the spiritual path. Abuse the body, and its life force drains away unnecessarily, limiting your abilities. I believe everyone can learn to see auras, listen to their inner intuitive guidance, and become more aware of the spiritual world around and within them. But to apply these things at a high level of proficiency and learn how to take these skills to the next level and really shine as a psychic takes significant amounts of energy and concentration.

Some of my favorite books about living a healthy lifestyle can be found in the bibliography at the end of this book.

The Effect of Drugs

I noted earlier that drugs can prematurely force open your doors of psychic perception and cause problems down the road as you try to develop your psychic abilities. You probably won't be surprised when I mention drugs are also harmful to the body.

Life offers us many opportunities to learn and grow. We set the pace for how much we gain from these opportunities by our level of interest, effort, and persistence. I understand how fun it is to relax and have a few drinks with friends, hang out at a barbecue, and play outside, and all the other ways there are to party and have fun. Respect the power of the new skills you're about to learn and understand it can be harmful to mix psychic abilities with artificial mind-altering activities. Over time, as you learn to seal your energy up before going out with a group of people who plan on getting drunk or high, you'll be strong enough to mingle with them without being negatively affected by their energy fields. For now, though, avoid such situations for a while.

Taking mind- or body-altering substances, from alcohol to heroin, affects the human energy field. In most cases we become more open to outside influences. Unchecked, we can actually absorb energy entering our personal space, including the auras of our friends, family, and strangers.

I'm all for having fun. I'm only sharing what I've observed our energy fields do under these circumstances. Developing psychic skills isn't like flipping a switch. If you're feeling called or inspired, even simply curious, to see if you can grow and develop your psychic abilities, understand that doing so moves you into a new way of being. Being psychic means drugs and alcohol are not your friends. Energetically, drug use creates problems that you could have otherwise easily avoided.

If you are on the spiritual path—truly, madly, and deeply in love with the spiritual path, with becoming a spiritual athlete, with gaining the strength and endurance to follow your spiritual path to the end and develop all the amazing skills you were born with—then you'll have the best results if you are sober. Being sober, your conscious awareness stays crisp and sharp, and a large part of developing your psychic skills is convincing yourself you're already *seeing* things. Your consciousness, however, is continually flicking these experiences off your radar of awareness. In order to bring these experiences more toward the center of your awareness, you need to expand your field of awareness. And drinking and drugs narrow your field of awareness.

Go out and dance, have fun, be goofy, and get stupid completely conscious and aware. Let yourself be fully present when you do fun things. You can still have loads of fun, and with your soon-to-be amazing psychic skills, you'll experience these situations in an entirely new way.

In particular, mind-altering drugs can actually retard your spiritual awakening. I have seen drug users with gray, cloudlike patterns in their auric field, usually around their heads but also across the chest.

Even people who consume mushrooms, typically considered a relatively harmless, naturally occurring substance, can develop a thick, gooey, yellow vibe through their auras following the shape of their bodies. I've also seen a type of unhealthy "greasiness" on the skin of drug users. Heavy drug users don't appear to be wholly themselves, and as I mentioned previously, I've often felt part of the spirit of the mushroom has merged with their auric field in an unhealthy manner.

People who trip on acid can develop a bright, glassy sparkle in their eyes. The sparkle appears very bright, like a light with no heat left. There's a "deadened vibe" beneath the sparkle. A much more lively brightness shines through the eyes of someone whose spiritual gifts are open. The acid spark doesn't have the health and vibrancy one sees in ordinary people. The shine looks sickly.

You can learn to solve your own life issues and answer your own questions about who you are, what you're doing here, and what your destiny is. You need to concentrate and work very hard to achieve solid results. Drugs slow your development, and in extreme cases prevent it altogether.

Drugs push your psychic senses wide open prematurely, sort of like kicking in a door instead of using the handle. If kicked open too hard or for too long, the door of perception won't sit properly on its hinges and may not ever close properly again. You will always be partly open to the psychic and spiritual worlds around you.

Just as our physical body picks up cues from the world around us via sound, light, touch, and other senses, so too does our psychic body pick things up in the form of energy. In most people, the process of sensing energy is automatic and unchecked. Our body's self-defense systems kick in when real danger is sensed, but otherwise we're left alone. Drugs can break these natural defense systems down and leave us open to outside influences, including the influence of other spiritual beings.

Spiritual beings come in all shapes and sizes, just like people. Some are good, some indifferent, and some harmful to humanity. From what I've observed in people, unless drugs are taken under the tutelage of a very experienced, usually extremely old and wise, traditional shaman(ess) or healer, doing drugs opens humans up to harmful spirits of low vibration. If you have no spiritual goals in life, then what you choose to do doesn't matter to you. But if you're embarking on a journey of spiritual discovery and trying to open up to your psychic abilities, then I guarantee you that it does matter. You do not want to mess with the low vibrational beings. Doing so is not fun, and it's not worth the pain and suffering.

We live in a sea of energy flowing together from high to low in a beautiful harmony designed to keep everything in its proper energetic station. Humans and angels don't normally mix because we're trying to learn different things from our experiences. If your psychic doors are blown open from drug use, then energy from out in the world flows in and your own energy leaks out. It can take years to heal the damage, and in the meantime it becomes difficult to keep out external influences at your discretion, especially in the dreamtime. You also harm the body's natural ability to experience spirituality, as well as its ability to store and digest these experiences. Negativity diminishes spiritual endurance moving forward and creates skewed or blurred insights.

One of the reasons to take care of the body is to increase your spiritual endurance. Just as athletes train to increase their physical endurance to play longer, so do spiritual athletes need endurance to handle extended periods of heightened perception. Drugs, in both cases, keep you on the sidelines. *The Way of the Psychic Heart* teaches you how to open up your psychic abilities without the use of drugs. Historically, among native cultures, drugs were used under the direct supervision of an experienced shaman or medicine person for specific purposes. Many drugs are addictive and historic teachers, who took on apprentices as adopted sons and daughters, never condoned indiscriminate drug use on a spiritual path. Drugs were never used recreationally.

In terms of our modern society, drugs are poisons. As the body reacts to, then neutralizes and assimilates, the poisonous substances of a plant, mushroom, or synthetic substance, hallucinations and other sensations are experienced. Just as excessive alcohol (another poison—to the liver) can weaken the body and mind, so do other drugs. When they are used too often, you can become dependent on drugs for visions, which is akin to going to the movies to watch other people's adventures but never going on your own.

To Be a Spiritual Athlete

What follows are several things to incorporate into your life in order to become a spiritual athlete. You do not have to do everything on the list religiously; the list is a guide. However, you'll be able to open to your psychic gifts more easily if you do more things on the list. The list is full of fairly simple strategies.

For example, eating unhealthy foods is harmful to the body and can also hinder your ability to concentrate, and keep you feeling lethargic or hyper-spazzed, either of which prevents you from taking care of things responsibly. Eating low-energy foods may also reduce your level of endurance, both physically and psychically.

The six simple principles you can incorporate into your daily life in order to become a spiritual athlete are: eat right, be responsible, practice regularly, be kind, build endurance, and schedule your workouts. Let's learn more about why these are important and how we can work them into our daily life.

Eat Right for Your Type

Food is an important part of a spiritual path. Keeping the body in optimal health gives you the energy you need to practice. Different people have different dietary likes and dislikes. I don't know if one particular way of eating makes sense for every person on the planet; some people are vegetarians, others are omnivores. No matter what appeals to you, be sure you aren't over- or under-eating for your body type. Eat the freshest foods possible. Minimize junk food; the preservatives and enhancers in these products can affect mental and physical strength and your ability to concentrate. The worst part about junk food is how it affects mood. Too much sugar or salt, even allergic reactions to certain ingredients, can make people cranky, irritable, and "moody." These mood swings can interfere with your progress.

Concentrating is an integral part of any spiritual practice. The simple act of eating right can make the difference between a positive or negative spiritual experience because food has a huge effect on our ability to concentrate. Eating foods high in salt and sugar can overstimulate the brain and body. We become too distracted to concentrate. If concentrating is difficult, review your diet and eliminate unhealthy or exceptionally stimulating food and drink. A dietician can be very helpful in sorting out your diet.

Vitality is another big issue for people. So many of us are tired no matter how much sleep we get. Rich, fatty diets high in animal protein take enormous amounts of energy to digest and can cause you to feel tired. Light, fresh foods like fruits and vegetables are energizing for the body.

For more information about healthy eating, consult the bibliography at the end of this book.

Take Care of Daily Responsibilities

Along with being a Good Householder to your body, strive to be one with everything you do in life. Spiritual exercises can leave you feeling high on life but ungrounded. The spiritual epiphanies people experience in deep meditation, or the amazing things you'll see in people's auras, can make the everyday world seem dull and unimportant.

I understand some people want to withdraw from the world in order to practice all the time. Spiritual epiphanies can become addictive. Where once you had to force yourself to practice, you now have to force yourself to stop. We are physical-spiritual beings, and enjoying all aspects of our reality in healthy and productive ways is fun. Becoming too material or too spiritual can lead to unbalanced human experiences, so remember to continue "being normal" even as your spiritual world unfolds.

A good way to stay grounded in the world is to get involved in work projects, socialize with family and friends, go climb a mountain, volunteer in the community, or find some other immersive activity requiring focus and attention. Where your attention goes, so do you. Pay attention to your body and life as well as your spirit, and enjoy everything life has to offer.

What seems mundane actually supports a rich spiritual practice. Pay your bills. Wash your dishes. Call your favorite relative. Be here in the world. The spiritual and material are designed to support each other and help each other become stronger. We can't choose one over the other because ultimately they are the same exact thing. Spiritual and material are simply two sides of the same coin.

Practice Regularly

No conscious activity yields results without practice. Consistency yields results. You don't have to be extreme; I've never heard of an Olympics for spirituality. Just apply the principles for taking care of the body to taking care of the spirit. If you want to develop your spiritual gifts, take a few hours a week and practice.

Keep things simple to ensure your success. Everything you practice will combine together, so do what comes easiest first. In the world of business, a common approach is to go after the "low-hanging fruit." Low-hanging fruit are ideas or opportunities easiest for you to achieve with the least amount of effort. Sometimes we shoot for the stars when what's really necessary is taking one more step forward. Go easy on yourself. You don't have to learn to slam dunk a basketball your first day on the basketball court. Start by learning how to dribble the ball. Life is much more fun when you are kind to yourself.

If it's impossible for you to relax your body but you have a cracker-jack intuition, practice developing your intuition first. The very act of practicing helps you to calm down. Eventually you'll master body-relaxation techniques, too. But whatever you do, keep practicing, and remember to also give yourself time to keep assimilating. You need downtime—unfocused time, as my wife calls it—to just do nothing.

The more you practice, the more you'll notice the quality of your downtime change. Whereas before you needed to go see a movie after spending a few hours meditating, later on after meditating you'll spend time walking through the woods in the presence of all the spiritual beings who live there. Your daily life and spiritual life become the same thing, to the point where your downtime is spent doing fun things with a spiritual twist, such as hiking through a forest and interacting with Nature spirits.

Be Kind

No matter what happens in life, you can always choose to be kind. No matter the chaos, there are always places of solitude and peacefulness. We cannot control the world around us, and the unexpected is often very commonplace. But we can always control the way we respond to the world around us. The choice is always yours. As the Dalai Lama says, "Don't let the world destroy your inner peace." Be kind. It's more relaxing and fun.

If you're quick to anger, take a deep breath and take a pause before saying something hurtful or reacting in any way to external situations. Say something kind to improve the situation; don't add gasoline to the fire. Yield to the situation. Be wrong. Be kind to everyone around you, including you. There's an old cliché about counting to ten before saying something mean. Taking a pause before acting out is a great way to separate your consciousness from a temporary fluctuation of irritation and anger.

If you think everything's your fault and feel guilty about it, take a deep breath and a pause and be kind to yourself. Maybe it's not your fault. Maybe it doesn't matter. Maybe you did the best you could; learn to be comfortable doing your best. You only compete with yourself.

No matter what negativity you're about to engage in, remember to take a pause in between moments of action and allow yourself the space to stop reacting and consciously choose to be kind. Breathe deep, relax, and just be in the moment for a second. Observe what's happening around you or within you. Find something kind about the situation as a beacon of light in your inner darkness. Allow kindness back into your conscious self and remember to choose kindness in each action. Do kindness. Say kindness. Be kindness.

Build Endurance

There are a few ways to increase your endurance along the spiritual path. The first way is learning patience. When I was a kid, I heard someone tell me the reward of learning to be patient is patience. Learning patience is its own reward. Perhaps you know this passage from the Bible: "Love is patient, love is kind" (1 Corinthians 13:4). This passage has deep spiritual truth. The actions we take to improve the quality of our spiritual path activates our heart center, and the more heart-centered we become, the more patient we naturally are.

The more love we feel in our heart, the more endurance we develop for our spiritual life. Love provides the increase in endurance. Love allows us to surrender to a given situation. When we surrender, there is no more grasping, hanging on, or resistance of any kind. Everything flows and there is infinite endurance.

Love is the key to a rich, deep, and meaningful spiritual path. Love connects everything in the universe together spiritually. A sense of connection keeps us in the present moment. When we're fully present, no endurance or patience is necessary. You're in the experience fully; there's nothing to wait for. There's nothing to hold or control, no need for endurance.

Being patient with things in your life creates a bigger space in between events in your life. Love exists in the pause between moments and builds endurance for everything coming our way in life. Love supports us through everything we undertake in life. Love really is the key to everything.

People who seek spiritual development as a means of securing power and developing their egos never learn about love. Power-seekers believe they'll get ahead by controlling their environment. Control could be focused on mind control, body control, pain control, emotional control, or any number of other types of control, including control of others. These hopes and dreams all stem from the mind, and it all evaporates upon the death of the mind with the death of the physical body.

For your own sake I pray you do not follow the path of power. You'll really be wasting a lot of time. Instead, surrender and yield. Be weak and soft. Humility prepares an inviting place for the heart. You can be confident and soft. You can be strong and yield. You can be fully present and engaged in life and yet be in a place of complete surrender, because you are surrendering to your higher self. Your higher self is the source of your energy, endurance, and strength. It stems from love, and so the greater your ability to love, the greater your capacity to commune and blend with your higher self.

Love more deeply to bring more energy and endurance to your spiritual endeavors. Patience is an aspect of a loving heart. The mind is quick; it gets impatient; it is primarily focused on your own needs before the needs of others; it has little empathy or compassion for the world at large. The heart is the opposite. It gives. It shares. It feels. It understands. It is present. Alignment with the heart is the best thing you can do to increase endurance as you travel your own spiritual road.

In concert with heart alignment are practices helping the body integrate spiritual energy for use later on. The number one thing I've done physically to help the body increase its ability to hold, digest, and use spiritual or psychic energy is to practice Chinese martial arts. Whether it's Kung Fu, T'ai Chi, Chi Kung, or any similar path of study, the Chinese system of martial arts is intimately aligned with energy flow, which in simple terms is called *chi*.

Chi is the same energy we use in spiritual practice. A good, traditional teacher integrates several martial arts training forms together to ensure you study a hard and soft blend of styles. A teacher who is focused on sparring and competition alone is not focused on the heart. Find a teacher who understands energy development and flow, and you have found a good ally along your spiritual path. Chinese martial arts naturally integrate into the human body without any mental effort. I'm amazed by how beneficial martial arts have been in my life.

Our next exercise is based on an exercise I learned from one of my former teachers. Similar techniques can be found in the works of Mantak Chia (see this book's bibliography for one of his books). The purpose of the next exercise is to increase the flow of energy through the body. Increasing energy flow provides more energy for us to use during the psychic exercises in Part II of this book, "Learning to See with the Three Pillars."

Exercise:

Helping the Body Integrate Spiritual Energy

Sit comfortably cross-legged on the floor with hands in your lap. If you need back support, use whatever props or supports are necessary to allow you to feel comfortable for the next fifteen minutes.

Take several deep breaths and relax. Allow your attention to be in the moment completely. Feel your body—your bones, muscles, and organs. Feel how your body is sitting on the floor, the temperature of the room, and any noises around you. Feel the weight of your hands lying comfortably in your lap.

Focus your attention on the area at the base of your spine near where your buttocks touch the floor. There is a major energy channel flowing through this part of the body. On the next inhale, visualize a warm glow of energy at the base of your spine being pulled up along your spine all the way through the back of your neck to the crown of your head. The energy may feel like shivers running up or down your spine. Such feelings are normal. Hold the inhale during the entire time the energy moves up your spine.

As you exhale, send the energy down the front of the body all the way past the pelvic region and back to the base of your spine. Those who could not feel the energy move were instructed to visualize it moving with their imagination, as we were told it moves whether we believe it does or not.

Continue the process of moving energy up your spine and down your front using the breath as a guide for about ten minutes. When you are ready to finish the exercise, the process is stopped by exhaling the energy down to your navel instead of the base of your spine. The energy is naturally absorbed and assimilated by the body. In traditional Chinese healing, the center of our being is located in the navel.

Continuous and regular practice increases vitality in the body. The technique can be done as its own meditation or incorporated into daily life activities such as reading or walking. I often move energy through my body as I drive. Obviously I can't cross my legs, but I can feel the energy flowing through me as I breathe.

A variation is to continue moving energy through your body with a second loop up and down your legs to bring the energy through all parts of the body.

Begin as before, sitting comfortably with legs crossed and palms in lap. The first inhale takes energy up the spine. The first exhale takes energy down the front of your body. Instead of bringing the energy back to the base of the spine, as the energy moves through the pelvic area, allow it to continue traveling down the back of both legs, all the way down to the bottom of the feet. The next inhale takes the energy from the bottom of the feet up the front of the legs, through the pelvic region to the base of the spine and then up the back of the spine to the top of the head.

Continue for about ten minutes. When you feel you are finished, bring the energy to the navel for digestion and assimilation.

One aspect of force in martial arts is called *jing*. Jing is the ability to focus your chi on a particular task, such as kicking or punching, but it also includes the ability to concentrate on things like meditating and spiritual *seeing*. Good jing makes a good fighter, but on a deeper, more meaningful level, it makes a good student. Moving energy through the body is an excellent way to build chi and generate good jing.

Schedule Your Workouts

There are many ways to schedule a spiritual workout. I like to set certain mornings each week for meditation, certain times each month to immerse myself in Nature to connect to my spirit friends there, and certain times each month to connect with my guides. Beyond my scheduled practices I stay open and present to other spontaneous spiritual experiences. Find a routine that easily fits in between your other life responsibilities. Be successful by being consistent in your practice.

When I was younger, I spent time after school practicing moving objects with my mind. Anytime I was near a thunderstorm, I practiced calling lightning down. Every night in bed I practiced seeing my aura, listening to my intuition, and other things, just to continue improving my skill level. Even though I have no desire to mess with the elements these days or try to use telekinesis, I was developing practice habits that continue to help me on my current spiritual path of meditation: talking to my guides or interacting with Nature spirits. Developing good habits early in your spiritual practice makes it easier for you to deepen your practice down the road.

No matter what your spiritual goals are, be consistent. Learning any skill, such as yoga or a foreign language, requires practice to learn. We live the truth of our limitations every day. We all have our peak moments, and we have all our low points. What the exercises in *The Way of the Psychic Heart* can do is help you increase your average skill level. If you want to develop it, you have to set aside time in your busy schedule and practice.

Being a spiritual athlete is simple to understand but takes time to achieve. Be patient with your progress and enjoy the unfolding process of spiritual development. To help understand how you're progressing, the following questions can be answered throughout your spiritual journey. Once each month, quarter, or year, devote a section of your journal to reflect on your experiences and your progress. Self-assessment is a great way to benchmark your achievements.

Quiz: Your Spiritual Athleticism

Answer the following questions to gauge your spiritual athleticism. Write pertinent answers in your journal to mark the progress of your spiritual transformations.

- Describe your current eating habits and overall lifestyle. How have they changed in the past six months?
- What lifestyle goals do you hope to achieve moving forward?
- How do your eating and other lifestyle choices affect your mood, energy levels, and overall outlook on life?
- Describe your career and other life responsibilities. How do you feel about them? Do they resonate with your personality and spirit?
- Describe your future life goals and dreams. How close are you to achieving them?
- How has your spiritual practice affected your ability to meet your everyday responsibilities?
- What goals have you set for the future to help you create a life more in alignment with your hopes and dreams?
- List ten things you love about who you are—the things the make you uniquely you.
- What positive things have you done for others?
- What things have you done to care for and honor yourself?
- List ten things you could do to increase kindness in your life.

- List the things you do to keep your body healthy and strong, such as yoga, swimming, or time spent at the gym.

Do you believe you are doing enough to keep yourself healthy and strong for the rest of your life? If not, what could you do differently?

Simply for reference and not from any sense of judgment or bias, write down how many times you did anything you consider spiritual in the last month, including things like going to church, spending time in Nature, meditation, or other heart-centered activities. When you see what you've been up to, how do you feel? How do these activities make you feel?

Create a plan for the near future and include all the things you'd like to do if you only had the time to do them. If you haven't recently done so, repeat the smudging exercise learned previously. If you've recently smudged, move on to the next step.

Reviewing everything you've just written or reflected upon, create affirmations and goals for the next month, quarter, or year of your life. Select the top five and read them aloud. Let the world know what you want to do, how you'd like to change, by saying a few things aloud.

When you're done, sit quietly for a few moments in silence.

Part II

Learning to See
with the Three Pillars

Chapter Three

Developing Awareness

I think self-awareness is probably the most important
thing towards being a champion.
—BILLIE JEAN KING

Grounding in the Body

Humans seem to be unique among living species on Earth. We are born incomplete like our plant and animal brothers and sisters. We are cared for by one or more parents, and our community teaches us many things, which is also very similar to the plants and animals with whom we share the world. But as we grow to maturity we remain incomplete. It is up to us as individuals to choose how to complete ourselves. Animals and plants find completion at adulthood. Naturally, development to full completion significantly sets us apart from the plants and animals with whom we live. Everything else in Nature grows up to its full potential. You never hear of a squirrel who couldn't figure out how to crack a nut, or a bear who never learned how to hibernate, or a tree without leaves.

But humans are different. We're each so unique; like fingerprints, no two of us are alike. Even twins have their differences. What sets us apart from other forms of life is our ability to change on a personal level. We have free-will choice. Society at large is there to help us grow into many things we could choose to become: designer, musician, athlete, teacher, parent, or business owner. The pull of external influences on our lifestyle, diet, or moral compass, for example, is powerful. We are at least partially a product of the greater society within which we live, but we also have our own unique flare to add to the mix.

Much of what we learn from our culture helps us to integrate and function with our fellow citizens in wonderful and productive ways. Excessive integration to the point of unconscious conformity can seem at odds with our spiritual life, which by its nature is more introverted and individualized. Caring enough to carve out time for personal growth is an important first step on the spiritual path. Ultimately, by spending time within, you emerge as a more productive and positive member of society. It becomes a win-win situation for everybody.

Your psychic development is connected to the rest of your life. You have a body, a mind, emotions, a soul, and a spirit that must work together in harmony as you walk through life. Therefore, be aware of your body and how it works. Too often I see people use "spiritual development" as an excuse to avoid the rest of their lives. I once overheard a woman say we are not our bodies and only the spirit mattered. The body does matter. Denying the body is just as harmful as denying the world of spirit and magic. The woman was very unhealthy. I felt she said those words to come to terms with her inability to control her body and health. Saying her body had nothing to do with her was a way to rationalize disrespecting it. Her spiritual philosophy went counter to her physical reality because she was ungrounded. Pay attention to your own self-defeating patterns. Becoming aware of self-defeating behaviors gives you a chance to make changes and become more balanced.

Increasing awareness, seeing auras, and developing intuition connect you to the larger parts of yourself. These are parts connected to the entire world around you. Plugging in to the world of energy connects you to the present, the past, and the future simultaneously. The only things limiting our ability to be psychically active all the time are our levels of conscious awareness and vital energy. If these were unlimited, we would be all-seeing and all-knowing. Our brains would only be used to regulate our physical processes.

Increasing awareness, seeing auras, and developing intuition work together to help us spiritually wake up more quickly. Through increased awareness, we notice the energy fields around all living things and pick up intuitive vibes more easily. Seeing energy fields on a regular basis increases our awareness. Listening to our intuition is another form of "seeing" energy patterns flowing in and around us, which improves our ability to see auras and other energy fields more easily. In a way, these are three aspects of the same thing. All we need to do is choose to listen and follow these higher parts of our consciousness.

Your psychic or spiritual abilities are directly related to the level and quality of your awareness. With increased awareness comes increased clarity. Clarity helps cut through imagination. The spiritual path is very subjective. Many things you experience cannot be verified physically. It's easy to be fooled by what you want to see rather than what's really happening because the spiritual path challenges the very notion of what reality is. Reality is where we live in the here and now.

Feeling completely present is called being grounded. People who are ungrounded can get themselves into all sorts of trouble. Whether tripping on a step, suddenly finding yourself in the wrong place at the wrong time, or worse, staying grounded keeps you protected as you walk the spiritual path. I hope all of your experiences are positive, but everyone's path is unique and some are pretty complicated. Jumping in head-first with your eyes closed can bring you in contact with some less-than-friendly spirits, disembodied ancestors, and other potentially unpleasant beings. Staying grounded helps prevent unwanted contact. Simply being aware of what is happening is often time enough to protect you from harm. Your body offers natural protection from many negative influences.

After practicing, bring your energy back completely into your body to stay grounded. Too much time spent being ungrounded can interfere with your ability to complete your daily responsibilities. However, keeping things tight and grounded keeps you focused in all areas of your life. You remain effective at manifesting your desires.

Carlos Castaneda writes in his books about how his teachers looked for potential apprentices among people who were already grounded and who wouldn't normally be interested in the spiritual path. People able to get along well in the ordinary world were already grounded and present and remained focused through the trials to come. His teachers avoided choosing people who yearned to become shamans because people trying to escape daily responsibilities were prone to being controlled by the powerful spirits they were soon to encounter.

From the perspective of *The Way of the Psychic Heart*, anyone can learn to become psychic, whether they're drawn to spiritual things or not. The point I'm making with the above story is that you'll have an easier time learning to open to your spiritual abilities if you also continue opening to your material abilities. Becoming psychic is a way to become more present, successful, and capable in the everyday world.

Those who go through life focused and alert are more productive and successful than those who aren't, whether at work or on the spiritual path. Being focused and alert keeps you in the moment, and those who are most fully present in their

bodies are best able to listen to, and have the willpower to follow, their intuition.

I've seen many students become overwhelmed with the
amount of energy available to spiritual seekers. Prolonged ex-
posure to intense energy can leave you feeling heady and lightheaded, dizzy and out of sorts. Even so, upon discovering we
really, truly live in a magical world—and not just through a
dream or imagination or creative visualization, but really magical here and now in daily life—people can be forever changed.
It could become all you think about, all you want to do; it could
become addictive.

Our world is full of amazing opportunities, positive growth
challenges, and special opportunities designed just for you. If
you become ungrounded, you may miss out on them. So be
here now. Earth is a good place to be.

Exercise:
Body Presence through Self-Observation

Self-observation is a simple exercise with a powerful
punch. Self-observation keeps you focused and in the
moment.

*As you make your way through the world, allow yourself to
feel yourself in your body. Feel each muscle, bone, and joint
as you climb stairs, lie down to bed at night, sit still while
watching TV, or argue with a co-worker. Feel the happiness*

of playing with a baby; feel your body in everything you do. How do you hold your head when you do your homework? What nervous twitches do you have and what triggers them? Do people trigger certain thoughts in you? How do these thoughts affect the tension or relaxation in your body?

Feel your sense of balance: Which foot is dominant? Which eye is dominant? Become aware of how you feel in different situations. As much as you can, observe to the tiniest detail how you live your life.

Observe yourself all the time; while driving, eating, watching TV, breathing, anything. Always be aware of how you feel in your body. Self-observation is an extremely simple way to increase your levels of awareness.

Learning self-observation is a challenging and powerful tool for self-transformation. Being aware 24/7 has some surprising side effects. Change unfolds in a very organic and natural manner. Life changes effortlessly. Random habits fall away. You feel the weight of your words, thoughts, and deeds before taking action, and otherwise feel a stronger sense of your conscience. Not a religious, guilt-based conscience, but something far more pragmatic and personalized.

Another helpful technique for becoming more grounded and present involves concentrating very hard on your body. Intense awareness of the body is a helpful technique—if you just finished a deep meditation and you need to go back out into the world right away, for example. It's not a gentle technique and can feel jolting at first, but the practice definitely comes in handy.

Exercise:
I Am Here!

The following exercise involves looking into a mirror and staring at yourself while saying a few words out loud. It's very important to be focused and feel yourself in your body.

You can perform this quick exercise anytime and anywhere you feel ungrounded—for example, when you wake up first thing in the morning. Head into the bathroom and look at yourself in the mirror. Look into your eyes and say aloud, "I am here!" while shaking your arms and legs a few times. Open your eyes and mouth as wide as possible. Really stretch your face out. You can even make noises. Splash cold water on your face. Repeat the same actions from the beginning. Now gently grip your hair and tug gently at the roots. Pulling your hair increases blood flow and oxygen to the head. Repeat these activities until you feel present and "in your body." The more confident you become, the more effective it is. Really say aloud with confidence, "I am here!" Own your space. Be in your body. Move through life awake, aware, and alive.

The more you practice, the more grounded you feel. The more you practice, the longer the effect lasts. The feeling of being completely present can last all day, all week, all month, and all year, until finally you only need to repeat the exercise occasionally.

Learning to Relax

Now we are going to deeply relax the body. However, combined with the previous practices of self-observation and maintaining body awareness with the "I am here" technique, relaxing the body can leave you feeling very refreshed and present. Let's practice.

Exercise:
Relax the Body

Performing a complete body relaxation is best done at night when you are ready to sleep. Talk to your significant other. Catch up on your reading. Do everything else in bed first and then relax the body.

If you need light, use a candle but turn off any electronic devices around you, including lights, as their electric fields can be stimulating to the body. Lie on your back in a comfortable position. Begin breathing naturally but deeply. Become aware of being in your body, in your bed. Feel the sheets and blankets on top of you. Feel the mattress below you. Notice any tension in your body.

Inhale deeply and hold the breath for several seconds. As you hold the breath, feel your whole body becoming more tensed. Let the breath out slowly and feel your entire body relax. Repeat several times, each time becoming more and more relaxed.

Note: Sometimes before you finish relaxing your body, you will just fall asleep. This is completely normal. Feeling sleepy means you were very tired and needed to sleep. Sweet dreams. As you rejuvenate your body through resting, you'll be able to continue on to deeper levels of relaxation. Try again tomorrow.

The next level of the exercise is to focus on individual parts of the body. On your next inhale, pay attention to your head. Feel the muscles in your face; where is there tension? Feel your scalp, ears, eyes, every part of your head. As you hold your breath, feel the tension in your head and face. Pay attention to the most tense area(s) and mentally say, "Relax" to those areas as you exhale. Feel the muscles respond to your suggestion and relax more deeply. Repeat several times until your jaw, throat, eyes, forehead, and all other parts of your head are relaxed.

Now move to your arms. Beginning on your left side, inhale and hold your breath and become fully aware of your entire left arm. Feel your fingers, knuckles, palm, wrist, forearm, elbow, all the way up to your shoulder. Feel any tense areas as you hold your breath. As you exhale, mentally say, "Relax" to those areas. Repeat until your left arm feels like melted butter, completely relaxed.

Repeat for the right arm.

Now move to your legs. Beginning on your left side, inhale and hold your breath and become fully aware of your entire left leg. Feel your toes, your arch, heel, ankle, calf, knee, and thigh, all the way up to your hip. Feel any tense areas as you hold your breath. As you exhale, mentally say, "Relax" to those areas. Repeat until your left leg also feels like melted butter, completely relaxed.

Repeat for the right leg.

Now move to your torso. Inhale deeply as you sense the entire torso. Hold your breath and feel any remaining areas of tension. Feel your spine and back, your sides, belly, and chest. Say, "Relax" to yourself as you exhale and allow all tension to fade away. Repeat until your entire torso is relaxed.

Sometimes after your body's muscles are completely relaxed, tension still exists in certain areas, such as a particular joint or the intestines. Repeat the same breathing process on your intestines as you did for your muscles. It may take several weeks of practice to completely relax, so don't worry if it stays tense for a while. Apply the same technique to any other tense areas of the body.

For the joints, inhale deeply and imagine the air you in-hale is full of bright white light. Hold the breath in the heart and smile. As you exhale, let the light breath move to any uncomfortable joints. Allow yourself to relax more deeply as the healing light works on your joints. You may feel a warm sensation or a tingling feeling. Specific sensations vary from person to person. Some say it feels numb as the pain fades away. Others say it just feels "normal" again.

The goal is to become so in tune with your body that you can deal with the tensions generated in your life each and every day. Practicing in bed when you're already relaxing is a safe place to learn deep relaxation. Deep relaxation prior to sleeping helps you feel more energized the following day. Holding tension in the body may lead to several types of de-bilitating health issues. Being aware of your body is the first step in becoming more aware of the world around you. After much practice relaxing your body, you learn to be in control of your body during stressful situations. Staying relaxed under pressure maintains your awareness and keeps you in tune with your intuition and other psychic abilities.

The more relaxed you become, the more easily you'll fall asleep and the more refreshed you'll feel the following morning. Feeling completely relaxed is a great feeling. Often, I woke up in the exact same position in which I fell asleep.

Increasing Awareness

You've learned to relax. The next step is to be able to stay alert while doing so. Staying alert and relaxed is an easy way to become more aware of the world around you. Most people wander through life lost in their thoughts, focused on their next task, and otherwise disconnected from and distracted by the world around them. Today's fast-paced culture makes it easy to live a distracted life. Remembering to stay relaxed and aware of our surroundings is something we can do throughout the day in a variety of situations. The more we practice, the better able we'll be to stay focused and present in life. The following exercise describes a simple technique to stay present.

Exercise:
World Awareness

No matter where you are or what you are doing, stop what you are doing and take a deep breath. With your awareness follow the breath in to your body and observe yourself. Start with the simple things. How do you feel? Where are you right now, inside or outside? Is there a breeze? Is the weather sunny or cloudy outside? Who else is around you? What are they doing? Do they feel tense or relaxed? Look up in the sky. What's going on up there?

When you are walking through your life, what plants are near you? What people? Do they have pets with them? How

does your body feel? Is the world around you noisy and dis-
tracting or quiet and peaceful? No matter where you are or
what you are doing, pay attention to everything happening
around you.

As with the Self-Observation technique, World Awareness gets you to pay attention. It's incredibly simple to do yet very difficult to incorporate into daily life. However, paying attention is a critical skill to learn if you want to be able to notice and remember any psychic experiences you've had. People commonly forget spiritual experiences and psychic events if their consciousness hasn't been trained to allow such experiences into their everyday reality. If our goal is to increase our psychic abilities, then we need to remember as much as we can from our experiences.

Old Memories

While developing your abilities and maintaining increased awareness, you may remember things long forgotten. Memories include important dreams about current or future events, memories of meetings with spiritual people or spirits, or other significant experiences. Write these events down in your journal in case you forget again.

Our lives run in cycles of interests, career and family choices, even the types of foods we like. The same is true of our spiritual life. We focus on spirituality for years and then move on to other things for a while, perhaps to focus on more worldly responsibilities such as work or family. During these ebbs and flows of our spiritual life, we tend to forget events from the past. Your journal can help you remember these events and inspire you to maintain at least some type of spiritual practice during these downtimes.

You have all the awareness exercises you need now to start on your path. Becoming psychic really isn't complicated. It's just a matter of doing the right things in the right order to condition your being to strengthen, and paying attention to what you're probably already doing. The more you practice, the easier it is to maintain a regular state of heightened awareness. One of the main techniques to develop your psychic gifts is increasing your general awareness—to get used to living in a heightened state of awareness. My belief is you won't be able to *see* much of the spirit world, whether your aura or an angel, if you aren't even noticing what's happening in the physical world you're already living in. Making efforts to increase your awareness is especially true if spiritual or psychic things don't come easily to you. Everyone can learn to *see*, and setting a good solid foundation built in awareness is immensely helpful.

The more present you are, the more details you notice. Eventually you notice energy patterns, spirits, auras, and other truly remarkable surprises. But you have to start with the three-dimensional world you were born into before you can move out into other realms. And you may be surprised to discover how many strange things you already notice once you start maximizing your awareness. Chances are you are already *seeing* things on some level, and living in a heightened state of awareness helps you notice them sooner than later.

You may not know if you're prone to becoming ungrounded until after you practice for a while. Maintaining your focus and attention in your body takes practice but is important if you want to stay engaged in everything you do. Grounded people have an easier time on the spiritual path. Grounded, practical people *see* more, have more endurance, are more functional between worlds, are better able to use their power of intention to manifest opportunities in their lives, and are more protected.

The following self-assessment quiz marks your progress. Refer back to these questions over time as you continue opening up to your psychic abilities. Your journal is a great place to keep notes and feedback on your progress.

Quiz: Breathing and Awareness

Answer the following questions truthfully. To track your progress every few weeks, check back in and see if your answers have changed.

Breathing

- Describe your success at relaxing your body and focusing on the breath. Has it been easy to achieve?
- What areas of your body remain tense when you try to completely relax?

- How is your breathing during the day? Has it changed or become calmer since you started your practices?

- Can you feel the effects breathing has on your muscles? Does controlled breathing help you relax more deeply?

- When you feel tense areas, can you relax them with breath?

- Do certain thoughts arise with specific tense areas of the body? If so, are you able to breathe the thoughts away and relax?

Awareness

- Describe your experience practicing self-observation, and then do the same for maintaining awareness of the world around you.

- Does living in heightened awareness come naturally to you? If not, what sorts of things distract you? Physical sensations? External sounds or other distractions? Write down whatever distracts you so you can focus on maintaining awareness when these things occur.

- How long are you able to stay aware of your surroundings during the day?

- Are you able to hold your awareness over your body all day long?

- Can you sense when someone is watching you and from where?

- Have you noticed any particular sensitivity to certain situations, anything you can easily pay attention to? For example, do you sense changes in people or a room before they happen? Sense a driver's intention before he or she changes lanes in traffic?

- Set a few goals you'd like to achieve in the coming month, quarter, or year. Make a list of the most distracting things in your life. Refer to the list as you start your day to stay aware of potential distractions. Awareness of a distraction is frequently enough to prevent similar distractions in the future. When you find yourself in a distracting situation, remember to stay present, breathe, and remain centered. Don't let the external affect your internal state of being.

Chapter Four

Seeing Auras

The aura given out by a person or object
is as much a part of them as their flesh.
—LUCIAN FREUD

Human beings have many tools of awareness at their disposal. We use the standard five senses of taste, touch, smell, sight, and sound to interpret the world we live in. But there are other forms of awareness at our disposal we can learn to develop with practice. The rest of *The Way of the Psychic Heart* contains exercises to help you learn to develop these additional levels of awareness. Other forms of awareness are completely natural and have nothing to do with any religious, philosophical, or spiritual worldview. Awareness exists, like vision and smell simply exist. With practice we can learn to expand how much awareness we use on a daily basis. You may already be using these other senses to unconsciously gather information about the world around you without realizing what you're doing. Heightened awareness exists beyond the scope of the brain and takes conscious effort to notice.

Learning to see auras was one of the best things I ever learned. I opened up to a whole new world. Once I learned to see my own aura, I noticed energy everywhere. I couldn't believe I hadn't noticed auras before. I saw auras around other people, but also everything alive. I noticed auras around plants and animals of all types. I also noticed auras around objects people had interacted with for a very long time, such as old houses, historical sites, and other things. Remember the story of the necklace I bought from the old man at the pow-wow? I even noticed aura energy around streams, clouds, fires, rocks, and other inanimate objects. Looking at the energies surrounding nearly everything in the world around me was a real eye-opener. Seeing auras made the world feel more alive than I'd ever imagined.

A side effect of seeing energy around living things is the ability to see the energy signatures of things your physical eyes can't see. Seeing spirits for the first time can be surprising, so if the idea freaks you out, you can tell yourself you aren't ready to see such things. The brain readily tunes out what you aren't ready to see.

The first sense you'll learn is seeing auras. What is an aura? Auras are energy fields surrounding all living things, including some things we consider inanimate, such as rocks and clouds.

Most people see auras as layers of pulsating colors surrounding the body like layers of an onion. We'll start by learning to see our own aura and then move on to seeing auras around other people and things.

People have recorded seeing auras for millennia, from images in rock art to ancient treatises on traditional Chinese medicine to many modern books on the subject. The introductory practices you've just learned, especially the exercises for learning to live with heightened awareness, are valuable tools supporting and enhancing the following exercises. If practiced diligently, the previous exercises help you see auras more quickly and completely.

The aura is the energy field we live in. Auras are a part of our physical body, less dense than our flesh and bones. Auras are an extension of our body-mind-spirit complex. Auras occupy the space of our physical body but extend beyond it several feet or more in every direction. Typically, the aura is shaped like an egg, though not always. Auras interact with the world around us much differently than the body or mind. And just like our other sensory and consciousness centers, the aura is already doing what it does, processing energy, keeping our body alive, and feeding us information about the world around us without our conscious knowledge of its process.

Auras are constantly processing interactions with the world around us and feeding us the information they receive. Information transfer happens nearly instantaneously, much too fast for the brain to think about. Our brains are pretty linear and think about one, perhaps a few, things at one time before moving on to the next thing. Auras are more like holograms, touching everything at once in a fluid and unrestrained manner.

Everything present on Earth has an aura of some sort. All humans, animals, plants, minerals, water, clouds, magma—everything has an energy field. The earth has an aura, too. Besides animals and humans, there are myriad other forms of consciousness. Native cultures learned to communicate with plants, stones, even the earth.

Learning to see auras is one of the most powerful psychic abilities because it is the gateway to so many other things. You'll learn to see spirits, ghosts, fairies, energy portals traveling to other places, other types of topography in the landscape and the sky, energetic signatures from past, present and even future events tied to a specific geographic area. Seeing auras allows us to receive vast amounts of information from their owners, and is a great way to learn to read people. Learning to see your own aura is a new way to learn about yourself and *see* what is happening with your mind, body, and spirit.

Each form of life has consciousness. It's amazing to experience the variety of personalities and psychologies contained within each form of life. Maintaining an open heart and keeping the mind as quiet as possible when you look into another being's energy field helps maintain a more clear and fluid connection. Rivers of information flow between you in an instant.

Ever-present fluid communication of memories, ideas, words, and deeds happens all at once in a profoundly organized way.

After you've learned not only to see auras but have also grasped the ability to receive information, images, thoughts, and feelings from auric energy fields, give yourself time to fully process and integrate what you've experienced. The aura constantly receives information as we walk through life. Some information is given to the brain to process. Over hours, days, months, and years, new information will come to you about a particular event in the form of thoughts, memories, or visual images. It can take the brain a long time to process what it's received from reading an aura.

Learning to see auras also trains you to live with one foot in the world of spirit. It's possible to see auras 24/7 as you walk through life. Combined with the heart-opening and awareness practices featured earlier, living your life seeing energy fields everywhere has a positive transformational effect on your worldview. Everything feels more connected. The hiccups and apparent mistakes of life appear to fit together energetically like a balanced, rhythmic flow of energy patterns. It's difficult to describe unless you've seen the energy patterns for yourself, but the ability to see the energies of life everywhere has a positive effect on your outlook. You learn to live a spiritual life as normal and not some sacred, far-off experience.

By seeing auras you realize we're all connected and we're all spiritual beings. There are no gaps in energy. Where a friend's aura ends, someone or something else's aura begins, including the massive aura of the earth. Everything living thing on the planet literally connects to everything else.

So how do we do learn to see auras?

Your Aura

You are trying to learn a lot of different and new techniques. These techniques take time to master, and one particularly helpful technique to learn is the ability to seal up your energy from outside influences. In the world of spirit, sealing up keeps you from being affected by influences outside your control, and perhaps even beyond your ability to detect. Therefore I recommend learning to see your own aura first, because you're already living with its influences every day of your life. You can work on your "seeing" skills and start the learning curve of receiving information from energy fields by practicing on your own.

Exercise:
Sealing Up, Version One

Sealing up refers to plugging any leaks in your auric field. When we use our psychic abilities, we make an opening in our aura and send energy out into the world. In the case of seeing auras, the act of looking out into the world at other living beings' energy fields involves sending lines of energy, so to speak, toward whatever we pay attention to. These lines of energy generally follow our line of sight, but a more advanced version of seeing auras involves doing so while meditating with the eyes closed and observing a person, place, or object not near you. The same energy lines extend from your being out into the world through an opening in your auric field.

Psychics, empaths, and other highly sensitive people can suffer from having their auric fields full of several openings at any given moment. These openings not only leak our energy out of our field into the world around us but also allow external energy in. If we're not paying attention to our surroundings, we inadvertently pick up energy from our surroundings not compatible with our auric field. To us the energy feels negative, though it may not be negative to the next person. We're all unique.

Therefore, seal up before engaging in these psychic opening exercises. The concept is to set the intention, similar to the affirmations we learned about earlier, to close any open holes in our field. Then, once everything's shut, we make a conscious decision to activate a particular psychic ability and stay alert and aware while we practice learning how to use our skills. When we're finished, we seal up again and go about our day.

The technique is simple and honestly works best if you believe it will work. It's similar to the fairy-tale concept "In order to see magic, one first needs to believe in it." Believing you can seal up your energy field allows your mind to believe it can happen, which strangely enough allows it to happen. The mind creates our reality by believing a particular thing is possible. The power of positive thinking, creative visualization, and other similar techniques is based on the same perspective.

Before engaging in any further psychic opening exercises, feel yourself in your body—every toe, finger, limb, organ, and sprig of hair. Feel fully present and in the moment. Stand up awhile to really get grounded and fully present. At first I recommend saying the following phrase aloud, but later on, once you've mastered the technique, you can simply mumble or think the words, "I seal up my energy field and protect myself from all harm. No outside influences affect me and I am fully conscious and aware of my energy field. I only allow influences of the highest good and greatest benefit for my soul into my personal space. So be it."

Feel your energy field around your body—front, back, either side, above and below your physical body—to pull in closer to you and contract a little bit. Visualize golden light surrounding and covering your body. The golden light seals all holes connecting you to the outside world. I always feel a *cap of energy flap over the top of my head and seal my thoughts from the world.*

The end. Your energy field is sealed up. While you are sealed, you are protected from negative energy coming into your energy field and you won't leak energy out into the world. You can still see energy and sense information. Your body wisdom continues scanning the vicinity and feeding you any pertinent information to keep you safe, but you no longer leak energy into the world through sieve-like holes in your energy field.

We are now ready to learn to see auras.

Learning to see your own energy field, especially while living in a heightened state of awareness, builds up your endurance to living in the spiritual world. The more you include the spirit world into your everyday life, the better. Your mind agrees being psychic is normal and allows all those expanded parts of your consciousness to flow together with your everyday life.

When we combine energy and awareness, we put ourselves in a position to experience the magical side of life. The more you bridge your awareness between two worlds, the faster your skills develop. The more you learn to seal up and live like a spiritual athlete, the faster you'll build psychic energy.

The human aura looks like a multicolored, multilayered living cloud hovering all around us. It lives and grows with us in life, and people who see auras can see these changes in people.

Auras are in constant flux and respond to every subtle emotional ripple and changing thought inside us. Auras are affected by the clothes we wear and the food and drink we ingest. Auras change with our mood, life experiences, and state of being each and every moment of our lives, whether we are awake or asleep.

Auras are like eggs, very ethereal and light eggs. We live within the aura, in the exact same space as our body but also extending away several feet into the space around our body. The aura doesn't begin at the body. It runs through our entire anatomy. Other cultures have incorporated the human energy field into their medical practices. An example of this is acupuncture, which uses needles to interact with our physical and energy bodies at the same time to bring healing and balance back into our lives. The needles are inserted into bridge points connecting the physical body with the light, shining auric energy. Connecting the points via needles allows the two phases of our existence to work together in harmony for optimal health.

People with whom we come into contact on a daily basis are unconsciously responding to our auras. Some people are unconsciously drawn to us, while others are repelled. Spontaneous reactions happen all the time. Compatible people instantly relax around each other. Even if two people have just met, they gravitate toward each other, their energy fields pulling them together. On the other hand, people who have conflicting energy feel uncomfortable around each other. Feelings of nervousness and general discomfort easily arise. Our body wisdom senses the flavor of the auras it comes into contact with, even though our brain remains oblivious. When we learn to see energy directly with our eyes or consciously sense it with our body, it brings a greater understanding to the different types of relationships we have with the people in our life. The everyday sense-verification of seeing auras with our eyes or feeling them with our skin trains the brain to accept such things as a normal part of daily existence. Over time you consciously access all the information your aura is receiving about the world around you. The ability to see energy at will is a very exciting and life-changing event.

Of course, you can also learn to tune energy out using the sealing-up exercise learned previously. Most of the time, you will choose not to tune in to other people around you. First of all, it does take vital energy to see auras or exercise any other psychic talent. There really isn't a need to constantly have your skills turned "on." It can be exhausting. Whatever you see needs to be processed. Moreover, even though your aura is regularly paying attention to what's happening in the energy fields around you, the observation is passive. Your aura's just checking the perimeter to make sure everything is safe. It's a very different form of seeing than when you really open up your psychic eyes and *see* the energy around you. There's a much larger exchange of energy and information and takes more energy to accomplish and, afterward, process. Finally, after you've been able to see auras for a while, the initial glamour fades and it becomes just another skill in your toolbox of senses.

An analogy is using our sense of sight to completely look at everything around us. Yes, being able to see is an amazing skill, but soon we only really tune in to and stare at what really interests us. It's the same with your blossoming psychic abilities. It's easier to go through life if you can choose when you want to *see* and when you want to tune out. Picking up information from a person without their permission is disrespectful. We should be able to live private lives and it's really none of our business what's going on with other people unless we're asked to look. Another reason to practice on yourself and the natural world around you before practicing on other people: you can learn to perfect the ability to see auras while remaining respectful of others' personal space.

Even so, when the time is right and someone asks you to look at their aura, much can be learned. For example, you can sense the state of health of the body and its organs. You can learn to see the aura in detail and zoom in on specific areas—the liver or kidneys, for example. Combining the ability to see auric energy with intuitive abilities can yield insights into how best to bring healing and balance to the body and its organs. I know of several doctors, physical therapists, masseuses, chiropractors, and other health professionals who quietly incorporate their spiritual gifts into their daily practice. Some are deeply religious, some are atheists, and some are metaphysical. All use their psychic abilities to enhance their healing capabilities.

By interacting with the aura, you learn to see thoughts and emotions, receive visual images of memories and information about past-life connections. You can see and talk to a person's spiritual guides and helpers, those disembodied spirits present with us from birth to death as advisers and counselors along the journey of our present life.

Learning to see auras is a gateway to many other things. Auras connect everything in the universe together because every organized structure has an aura. Everything is alive, even solar systems, galaxies, galaxy clusters, and universes. Each collection of matter has a cohesive energy field, all the way down to the micro-scale, too. Each cell has its own auric signature you can learn to read in order to learn more about yourself and the world around you.

Auric energy connects everything in our solar system together. When the sun exploded into life and formed itself and the many planets, asteroids, and other heavenly bodies in our solar system, our home planet was also born. All matter, including us, lives within the energy field of the sun. Since we're all connected we can "plug in" and get information about anything we want or need to know about within the solar system.

Granted, achieving this level of skill takes years of practice. In this book we're learning the basics, and for us that means learning to see auras around our own body. Developing spiritual gifts is just like any other talent and improves over time with consistent practice. Anyone can learn to *see*, but some learn faster than others.

I have taught many people to see auras using the following techniques. A common reaction when people see auras for the first time is, "Oh. That's the aura? I've seen it plenty of times." Without a reference point to confirm what an aura looks like, without someone saying, "That's your aura and it's normal to see," some people don't realize they already see energy.

Receiving Auric Information

While looking at auras, we sometimes spontaneously receive information; this can be more common when we're still learning to seal our own energy field. So, what do we do with information we randomly receive?

A hard and fast rule is you don't give people information unless asked. We are not responsible for giving out information to people. One of the goals of *The Way of the Psychic Heart* is to give you all the tools necessary to *see* so you can receive your own answers.

Learning to see energy fields increases your intuitive abilities and vice versa. Over time your intuition becomes stronger and stronger, and you learn how to understand the information you've received. Sometimes, other people's spiritual guides are eager for their messages to be heard. Spirit guides really want to communicate with you. Spirit guides are under the same rules about not helping unless asked as we are. However, some spirit guides can be a little creative in their interpretation of the rule. When a psychic approaches the energy field of a spirit guide's ward, the guides may try to communicate with the psychic. People with open energy fields may also pick up information another person's guides are trying to convey to that person directly. Because you're open energetically, you're able to listen in on the conversation, so to speak.

If you feel you received the information accidentally, then go through the sealing-up routine as described and ask your own guides to only show you information about your surroundings with a direct bearing on your own life. If you feel you received information directly from someone else's guides and you do not wish to get involved in that person's life, simply tell the person's spirit guides to leave you alone. Guides are required to listen to your intention. Again, go through the sealing-up technique described previously and go about your day.

I was recently at a dinner party where a man began telling everyone what he saw or heard or felt about them without asking permission. He was an older man but had only recently learned to open up to his psychic abilities. Needless to say, he caused a lot of uncomfortable feelings at the dinner table. On some level it had the feeling of airing people's dirty laundry in public. It is wonderful to be able to see things once veiled from our understanding, but allow other people to open at their own pace. Life is not a race or a contest, and people need the freedom and peace to live their own lives at their own pace. In my youthful ignorance I enjoyed the rush of being right about my psychic insights, as I had no teachers to provide feedback if I was doing something right or wrong. Life experience was my only guide, and it took me many years to keep my aura sealed up and my mouth closed when it came to things of the spirit.

Learning to See Auras

Learning to see your own aura is fun. It's a great way to experience a psychic ability, and a safe and positive way to teach the mind to accept psychic reality. I teach people to see their own aura first because it gently retrains the mind to see a wider range of perception. Seeing auras combines well with the Body Presence and World Awareness exercises in chapter 3 because all three reinforce the importance of living in a heightened state of awareness.

Watching our own energy field in the safety of our own home is very nonthreatening for the mind. Forming little agreements with our mind that being psychic is normal adds up to big changes in our spiritual practice over time. Making efforts in a regular manner keeps the concept of expanded realities in the forefront of our thinking and helps transform our mental states of perception into something beyond our wildest imaginations.

There are many ways to learn to see auras, and no matter which method resonates with you, I recommend learning to see your own aura first. Only after getting good at seeing your own should you practice seeing other people's auras. I recommend keeping things personal for the same reason. Protect and bless your personal living space before engaging in spiritual practice. Looking at other people's energy opens you up to them. If someone has an energy field heavier or denser than yours, or full of hidden mental or emotional pain and suffering, you expose yourself to their energy, too. Until you learn more advanced ways of filtering information from the energies in the world around you, it isn't necessarily safe to practice on other people. When you are ready to look at other people's auras, start with close friends and family, those people whom you know the best.

In the world of spirit, simply paying attention to something creates a link between the two of you. Don't try to *see* unless you know how to shield yourself or otherwise break the link on a moment's notice. Practice the shielding exercise anytime you go out into the world. The technique is fast and accustoms you to staying aware of your personal space, owning your personal space, and feeling how your energy field interacts with the world around you.

Experience is the best teacher. Over time you will move from watching your own field to watching others' fields. Just walking through the world, you'll see auras around other people and things. With your energy shielded, looking at the energy fields around you is completely safe and no different from noticing things around you with the peripheral vision of your eyeballs. In chapter 8, "Spirit Guides," we learn how to make contact with the spiritual beings who watch over us as we live our life. These benevolent beings also help protect and shield us from harm.

What follows are some aura-seeing techniques I've discovered. Best of luck to you, and if you don't get to see your aura the first time, keep trying. The second exercise here, in particular, has worked for the many people I've trained over the years. Remember: practice, practice, practice.

Exercise:
Candle Meditation

Find a quiet, comfortable spot in which to practice; a candle and saucer to catch the dripping wax; and your journal. Find a comfortable place to practice and gather any pillows or other back supports. Find a nice, quiet area where you can be alone and relax. Bless the room as described in chapter 1's Owning Your Space exercise and then set the candle in front of you. The candle can be anywhere from six to ten feet away, on the ground or as high as eye level. Light the candle and turn down any other lights in the room so the candle is the brightest light in the room, though the candle doesn't have to be the only light in the room.

Sit six to ten feet from the candle in a comfortable position. Sitting in half-lotus style, with your legs crossed in front of you, is the best for energy flow, but be sure you are comfortable. We want to be relaxed so our concentration isn't distracted by the body's aches and pains. Take several deep breaths and become centered. Where are you? Where is your body? How does it feel? What are you wearing? What's happening in the space around you? Be fully present.

With eyes half closed, gaze at the candle's flame. Breathe in and out and practice relaxing your body in a sitting position in the same way you learned to relax lying down in chapter 3's exercise Relax the Body. As you relax more and more deeply, continue gently gazing at the candle flame. Watch the slow flicker of the flame and just breathe. Let every muscle in your body relax. Let your vital energy flow smoothly throughout your entire body. Keep your eyes open and focused on the candle flame. Watch it flicker and twirl with the subtly shifting air in the room.

Eventually you may notice a white glow around the flame itself. Where the fire of the flame ends, the aura of the flame begins. The candle's yellow flame blurs at the edges into a yellowish-white haze before fading into a pure white glow around the flame. The glowing light is rounded and has multiple layers. The layers are the energy field of the flame. Observe the layers. Pay attention to the candle as you have learned to pay attention to everything else happening around you. Move closer to better help you inspect the candle's energy field. If moving breaks your ability to see the candle-flame layers, start the exercise over. Really inspect the layers of energy around the candle flame. If you don't see anything yet, don't worry. Describe the qualities of the layers you do see. Remember the look and feel of the layers as a reference point.

In the dim light hold out your arm until it is within your peripheral vision. Continue staring at the candle flame and its energy field and slowly move your arm up and down at the edge of your peripheral vision. You may see a wave of color or white energy from your peripheral vision floating around your arm. Slowly shift your gaze from the flame to your arm by bringing the arm in front of the flame. As you gaze at your arm, look for a similar glow of energy around your arm to the one you saw around the flame. Notice any layering you see or any other eye-catching colors, patterns and shapes. If you can't see any energy fields by looking at your arm directly, then continue observing your arm from the corner of your eye using peripheral vision.

When first learning to see energy, the eyes and the mind are easily distracted. Using the candle flame as a neutral reference point can help your mind accidentally see the aura around your arm. The more you practice, the easier it will be to see your aura even while staring directly at your arm.

If you can see your aura around your arm, expand the view to look at all parts of your body by trying to concentrate *on seeing everything within your peripheral view. Continue studying the different layers and observe any colors or other distinctive features of your auric field. Remember to stay relaxed and keep breathing. Your thoughts follow your breath. Keep the breath calm and you'll keep the brain calm and relaxed. Let thoughts flow in and out like breath. Thoughts are not needed in any of these exercises. Stay in the moment and gaze at your aura. If the mind wanders by questioning what you're seeing, worrying you aren't seeing anything yet, or thinking about other things, you will have greater difficulty seeing auras.*

Practice the different ways of using the candle flame to help you see your own energy field until you are ready to stop. Write down any notes in your journal. At first I became easily distracted and lost sight of my aura. Even blinking made the vision disappear. After some time I learned that focusing on my peripheral vision was the best way for me to start to see my aura. As I continued practicing I was able to bring my arm nearer and nearer to the center of my field of vision. I also learned to see energy despite blinking, randomly shifting my eyes about the room, or other distractions.

When I finally saw my aura by staring at it directly, I noticed several distinct layers of less and less dense energy emanating from my arm out several feet into the space around my body. I noticed a very thin layer right next to the skin, a layer very different from other aura layers. The layer had no color; in fact it looked like the absence of color. As I understand it, the layer is the interface between the physical body and the aura. I used to call it the "black hole," because it looked like the absence of energy. I noticed if I put the very tips of my fingers together and then slowly moved them apart, the thin black-hole layer stayed connected between the fingertips. The energy fields surrounding my hands merged and flowed away from the black-hole line of energy that connected them together. After a certain distance, the connection broke. The second method for learning to see auras is based on observing the connection.

The second technique works best outside at dusk, after the sun is down but before night falls. The technique works even better if the sky is slightly cloudy. Weather brings a heightened electromagnetic charge that makes it easier to see auras. Even if you can't see colors right away, the energy around your body should stand out against the dull, gray background of the evening sky. If for some reason you can't go outside, then find a white wall in dim light and a similar effect may occur. Dress for the weather and head outside!

Exercise:
Hand Focus

The hand focus technique is very simple. Go outside at dusk, after the sun has set but before dark, and hold your hands up to the sky. Curve your fingers inward until all fingertips touch (not finger pads, but fingernail to fingernail). Don't worry about your thumbs, and if you have short pinkies you can skip them, too. Slowly pull your fingertips apart and look for a little line connecting the tips of your fingers together as you separate them, the line described previously. When you see the little lines connecting your fingertips, move your hands about six inches apart. Even small movements help you see energy bands around your fingers.

Keep slowly moving your hands closer together and farther apart until you see a hazy glow or trail of energy following your hands as you move them farther apart. The glow is your aura around your fingers. At dusk the hazy cloud of energy can look blurry, fuzzy, misty, foggy, or otherwise soft compared to the hard lines of your body.

Remember to move your fingers apart slowly; give your psychic eyes time to see the energy fields in front of them. Also experiment with moving your hands toward and away from your face; arms-length may be too far to see anything at first and nearly touching your face isn't very effective, either. Find the energy emanating from your hands. If it's easier to see one hand versus the other, drop one arm by your side and concentrate on the other one as you keep your hand held up to the evening sky. Allow your vision to see the energy band extend around your entire hand, arm, and finally your entire body.

At first you may not see colors, only white. The experience is different for everyone. Some people see colors right away. Some people see faded colors like a transparency over everyday life. And some people only see white their whole lives. The more you practice, the more you'll see. Try to see your aura around your entire body. Observe how the colors change, the way the aura is broken into layers of energy, any things existing within the aura such as objects or bands of energy cutting across different layers. The more comfortable you become seeing and understanding what's happening within your own aura, the more you will learn about yourself. Just looking at your aura may provide you with information about your health, happiness, and personal history having an influence on your current life.

When you are finished practicing, you may see auras around many things your eyes focus on. We all have a certain amount of psychic energy available to us each day, similar to the fluctuating energy levels of our body. When your psychic energy is depleted, your psychic sight naturally fades away until you've had some rest. If you want to conserve energy to practice again later in the same day, seal your energy field to turn things off.

Once you're comfortable seeing energy fields around your own body, try seeing the auras around trees. Tree auras are easy to study because they are so easy to find. Tree canopies also poke up into the sky at dusk, which makes their auras easy to see when you're first starting out. Trees also generally have very clean energy fields, which make them a safe target to view, especially if you are still learning to seal up your energy field.

Exercise:
Trees Are Alive

When you're ready to look at something besides your own aura, the next best things to observe are trees. Learning to see auras around trees helps you look at auras in the world at large. And while you're perfecting your ability to see your own aura, and before you look at any other animal or human energy fields, you can practice your external vision on trees. I don't recommend practicing on other plants, as certain plants have very strong, potent energy fields and may not understand why you're probing into their energy fields. From my worldview, many things have high levels of consciousness besides humans, which becomes apparent when we contact other living things with our psychic senses. Plants have distinct personalities and can be very powerful creatures. Trees have a slower and gentler "vibe" and are very patient creatures.

You'll be outside at dusk so dress accordingly. If the sky is too bright to see auras in one direction, then adjust your position until the energy field of the tree or forest pops out against the background sky. As I mentioned, energy fields seem easier for people to see at dusk. A tree's aura stands out against the background of the day's fading light.

If the trees are at the horizon, you can try and look at the entire canopy. If you're standing right next to a tree, even during winter, pick out a single branch or leaf cluster at the end of a branch. Condition yourself by staring at your own hand against the fading light until you see your energy field. Then shift your gaze to the tree or branch you've selected and attempt to see the energy fields floating around them.

Trees' auras have layers, too. See if you can discern their layers and the colors each one has. You'll soon find different tree species have different energy patterns. Certain evergreens are very electric blue and bold and seem to statically hug the shape of the tree, while others' auras extend in massive waves high above the physical size of the tree itself. With experience you can learn a lot about trees by looking at their auric fields. You pick up information about health, personality, memories, and other things.

Interacting with the living things of the world by opening a connection from your auric field to theirs is a way of communicating as foreign to our conscious minds as dolphins' sonarvision. With practice you can learn to use your ability to communicate as comfortably as talking out loud.

With practice you will be able to form your own perspective on the energy fields around living things. After you become comfortable shielding and protecting your personal space, you can communicate with a vast array of life forms while remaining safe and protected. Each experience builds upon the last to create a strong foundation upon which future experiences are based.

After several months' practice sealing up, seeing your own aura, and finally seeing trees' auras, you may feel comfortable enough with your skills to tune in to the auras of people around you. Always ask permission; perhaps you can practice seeing auras with a friend. As you gaze into each other's auric fields, share any information you receive as a way of verifying what you see against the realities of the physical world. If at any point you or your partner become uncomfortable with the practice, simply perform the sealing-up exercise and disconnect your energy fields by saying aloud that the practice time is over.

Remember to keep track of your experiences in your journal. Things fade with time and sometimes the greatest lessons are in the details of the information you receive from the world around you.

Once you've plugged in to the larger world around you, the world of lighter energy connecting everything together, you are free to explore as much as or as little as you wish. Several people I know incorporate their ability to see auras with their healing work as doctors, massage therapists, and counselors. Other people choose not to practice much, happy to see auras once but not interested in a lifetime of openness. Developing your talent is essential to having a positive experience with exercises featured in many other chapters.

Quiz: Seeing Auras

The following self-assessment gauges how well your skill is developing. Answer the same questions each month, quarter, or year and write down the answers in your journal. Regular self-assessment benchmarks your progress and helps you realize how your skills improve over time.

- What do you see when you see the aura? Do you see colors? Which ones?

- What have you practiced with so far? Seeing your own aura? Seeing trees? Other people? Recognize your attempts in your journal.

- Have you tried to see auras around plants or animals yet? If so, what did you see?

- When you do see auras, have you been able to receive any information? What types? Have you been able to verify your experience in the everyday world through any type of research or by asking questions of the person whose aura you studied? How accurate were you? Is there a particular type of information you receive—for example, always health-related or always about an event from the past?

- What are your short- and long-term goals for learning to see auras?

Chapter Five

Honing Intuition

Trust instinct to the end,
even though you can give no good reason.
—RALPH WALDO EMERSON

Are you familiar with intuition? Have you ever experienced an intuitive insight? Most people have at one time or another. You start thinking about somebody, and they call. Someone is speaking to you, and you know without hesitation they're hiding something from you or lying. In its simplest form intuition is the ability to know something you don't have evidence to support. We simply know something for no apparent reason. It's been portrayed as simple coincidence or excellent body-language interpretation, but in truth our intuition is feeding us information about the world in which we live.

The Subtleties of Intuition

Intuition is only as good as the practitioner. It doesn't always work for us because in large part having a strong intuition runs parallel to remaining calm in life. The more agitated we are, the less focused we feel and the harder it becomes to hear what our intuition is trying to tell us about a situation. I believe intuition is the wiser, more spiritually awake part of my deep unconscious self than my everyday self. Every human has the same connection with their intuition. One of the goals of embarking upon a spiritual path is to merge our everyday conscious self with our higher self and learn to live in both worlds simultaneously.

Because intuitive guidance derives from our higher self, I believe our intuition is always right. By its very nature, intuition cannot be wrong; intuition, and our soul, exists in a place of clarity. The part of us always connected to higher spiritual truth has nothing obscuring its vision. Intuition is clear and accurate, but our perceptual filters block our ability to accurately hear our intuitive guidance. Our mind wants a certain answer, which clouds and obscures the natural flow of intuitive information. Our hopes and fears befuddle the calm sensibility of our intuition, and we no longer feel confident about the answer our intuition is showing us. There are many distractions preventing us from tuning in to our intuition correctly.

Gurdjieff, the mystic I mentioned earlier in the book, saw all life experiences as "food" for us to learn from and digest.

Through the practice of self-observation learned previously, we learn to notice our patterns, and we learn to see the patterns in our life distracting us from staying centered, from living from our core. Self-observation spiritually "digests" our life experiences. Once life experiences are digested, the experiences become energetic food that fuels our spiritual growth.

The modern world of technology we've created offers many distractions and can encourage us to live a mind-centered life, where our thoughts flit quickly from one task to another. Having a strong and reflexive mind is a positive strength as long as it remains in balance with the other things making us who we are. We also need to maintain a strong and healthy body, as discussed in chapter 2, "Spiritual Athletes," and we need to have a healthy emotional life, strong and calm. We become immune to the near-viral levels of distraction present in the world around us.

Making efforts toward fostering a healthy mental, physical, and emotional being may seem to be a difficult and time-consuming series of tasks, but really is no more time-consuming than anything else we choose to focus on. Life at once gets in the way of our spiritual life and provides the exact opportunities we need. These apparent distractions are the food of which Gurdjieff spoke. Living relaxed and calm during the intensities of everyday life requires effort and concentration, but the tension builds endurance for spiritual exercise. Meeting the challenges of life head on in a calm, clear manner also increases our daily allotment of psychic energy each day. Much psychic energy is spent while engaged in stressful activities. When we learn to see work, family time, or learning a new skill as opportunities for spiritual growth, when we learn to see them in a positive light, we are able to release the stress. We get to keep the energy we once spent reacting to them for our psychic practice.

Take the Pause

The growth of our intuition is inversely related to our stress levels. The more we're stressed, the harder it is to hear our intuition. We become distracted by external incursions on our inner world. Therefore, it is important to learn how to stay calm in the face of stress, to keep our minds focused on the task at hand, and to maintain a heightened awareness of our surroundings and inner workings.

Staying calm under pressure creates space to hear our inner intuitive voice speaking to us, guiding us. When this calmness is combined with a focused mind undistracted by external stressors, we are able to remain aware and alert. This state of alertness is important because we need to stay alert and aware in order to hear our intuition. If the mind is splintered by focusing on all the stresses in our lives, then we lose that sharp edge in our consciousness that is required to hear our intuition. Intuition can be a subtle and quiet voice at first compared to the loud distractions of everyday life. In this chapter we'll explore how to create space in our lives to hear our intuition speaking to us by learning to stay calm, focused, and aware.

Living with clarity means you'll be able to hear your intuition faster and with more accuracy. The best way to increase clarity is to learn to take a pause during our hectic lives. Taking a pause brings us back into the present moment, and the best way to cultivate this is with the breath. Take a deep breath and gently hold it as long as you comfortably can. Then wait a minute before doing or saying anything decisive about a situation you're facing. The act of consciously pausing between actions separates you from the stress at hand and brings you back to your center, the home of your intuition.

With our intuition or our memory, the more distracted we are when asking ourselves a question, the harder to hear or remember the answer. It's not complicated. We are all supposed to have access to our intuition. And while certain forms of intuition are an acceptable part of our current culture, such as a mother's intuition, the only difference between memory and intuition is we don't typically practice using our intuition. So let's choose to practice!

Intuition is almost as vague a term as saying someone is psychic. Intuition is the most commonly used psychic ability in our daily life yet remains the most obscure aspect of the psychic tradition. Sometimes people are able to tune in intuitively and sometimes they're not. Sometimes intuition tells you someone is lying, and another time you'll fall for something hook, line, and sinker and never see it coming.

Much inconsistency is due to how distracted we are, but some inconsistency comes from various levels of natural talent. I believe psychic abilities run in families. Some have more psychic abilities and some have less, but all of us can learn to grow our skills, just like we can all learn basketball but only some of us play professionally.

Intuition is a very personalized skill for another reason. Even though the majority of the time intuitive insights come from our higher selves, there are times when what we understand to be intuitive guidance is actually coming from our spirit guides or from other factors in the world around us. All of these factors affect the quality and consistency of the information, as well as what parts of the information we're best able to understand. For example, if someone is better at intuiting things about the past, information they receive in a particular situation will focus on how past events shaped the present situation, whereas someone who is also good at reading auras may find their intuitive insights derive from the thoughts of the person the intuitive insight pertains to—thoughts that were seen as energy waves in the aura.

The way we receive psychic information can be very vague. Learning multiple ways to *see* allows you the opportunity to understand what works best for you.

Another difficulty with learning to develop your psychic abilities is that there's no pass/fail system to gauge your skills without some sort of external verification. In contrast, when you learn to see auras, you definitely know you're seeing auras. There is no confusion. Yesterday you couldn't see them and today you can. If you have an intuition about the future, however, you have to wait for time to pass to see if you are right. If you have an insight about another person, you either have to observe them or talk to them to see if your insight was correct. There's usually no immediate gratification.

Information gleaned through intuition is always filtered through the language center of the brain. Intuitive insights appear lightning-fast and are then processed more slowly by the brain. During processing, the brain analyzes information, weighing and balancing claims made by our intuition against what it thinks it knows to be true based on past events. The brain often slides its own ideas about things into the intuitive insight and modifies the information before you become fully aware of what's happening.

The practices that follow teach you the different "flavors" between intuition and thoughts. Learn to discern between these two sources of information to achieve greater clarity for your intuitive abilities.

Another way to increase the quality and consistency of your intuition is through meditation. Meditation naturally quiets the mind. When we learn to exist calmly in the world, we can also learn to minimize our thought processes during the day. We learn to live a more visual and holistic life not driven by the linear process of thinking. When meditation becomes integrated into our life habits, our intuitive insights come to us directly without filtration, in a flash, and whatever truth we receive is laid bare completely and wholly. Our decision-making abilities are lightning-quick with high accuracy. As the mind and body relax, our psychic and spiritual life accelerate.

The Difference between Thought and Intuition

The brain is an organ, like the heart or lungs. Our consciousness is not a result of our body. Our consciousness comes from our soul. I keep reading about people who want to download their brain into a robot and live forever. They don't realize we are already immortal: not in our body, but in our soul. The world in which we live is just a big playground. We're supposed to be having *fun* down here. (See chapter 11, "The Joyful Life.") Our consciousness comes from our soul, not the chemical soup we've temporarily borrowed from Mother Earth called the human body.

So then, what is the purpose of the brain? The primary function of the brain is information processing, storage, and retrieval, but also body regulation via interaction with the glandular system. The stuff we see, hear, touch, smell, and taste gets processed by our amazing brains. I think people are so attached to the idea of our center of consciousness is our brain because of the position of the eyes on our body.

Another group of information the brain processes throughout our lives is intuitive insights. Intuitive information, in contrast to what we receive from the five senses, comes to us with no logical explanation. We just know, we feel, or we remember something we never experienced directly. There's no boundary on instant knowing. Any topic is possible. You could suddenly know something about you or people you know, people you don't know, the history of a particular piece of land, a sudden remembering about the properties of a plant, or anything else you experience in life. Suddenly you just know.

Developing your intuition is akin to learning to speak and walk for the first time. Through these skills we catapult forward into a larger world and can suddenly participate in life more fully. Similarly, your first steps along the spiritual path connect you to the larger spiritual world around you, and you can also participate in life more fully. The better your intuition, the more connected you are to your higher self—the real, true *you*.

Give yourself time to develop a strong connection to the spirit world. You may spend years or decades following your spiritual path before you feel a solid connection to spirit. We're only as good as our ability to maintain a heightened level of awareness. Our intuition is fallible, and we stumble like a child first learning to walk. Our intuition is only as good as our connection with our higher self. As long as we rely on our physical brain to process information, the chance for error exists because the brain isn't using all the facts to draw conclusions about reality.

Intuition is our ally and never lets us down. Intuition is full of information and can be crucial to us living in harmony with our soul's desires, with our destined path through life. There's nothing better than living life in partnership with your intuition.

So how do we better partner with our intuition? How do we learn to receive its guidance?

I made up a game to help me feel the difference between my thoughts and my intuition. Learning the difference between the two was instrumental in helping me develop a strong intuition. I call it the "Yes/No game."

The Yes/No game came to me after I'd been practicing the Relax the Body technique from chapter 3 for some time. I became aware of subtle shifts in my body caused by different types of thoughts. Some of these shifts were basic, such as when my neck muscles tightened if I was stressed about something. But others were new to me and happened when I was doing something related to my psychic abilities. For example, I noticed the center of my abdomen felt calm and warm when I felt very confident about an intuitive insight. When I inhaled to relax my body, thoughts fluttered up in my head. Conversely, when I exhaled, it was much easier to stop thinking.

By learning to focus on sensory differences between my thoughts and my intuition, I learned to discern between the two. Each had its own flavor, character, and quality. Learning about the unique flavors of my thoughts versus my intuition allowed me to discern the differences between my thoughts and my intuition. I really wanted to remove any doubts about what information I was following to guide me through life. Was the answer coming from my mind's thoughts or my heart's intuition? The following Yes/No exercise was my solution.

I decided to only ask myself questions with either a yes or a no as the possible answer. I use only yes or no questions because I don't want to sort out a "maybe" answer with follow-up questions. If I got the answer right using my intuition, then I was really listening to my intuition. But if the answer was wrong, it must have been my thinking/imagination because I believe intuition comes from a higher, more spiritually refined part of human nature. I also believe intuition is always correct. Learning to feel the flavors between thought and feeling was the key to refining my intuition. Once I understood how to sense these flavors, my ability to listen to my intuition improved. I was less confused by the mind's tendency to analyze and weigh the pros and cons of each side of my question in an attempt to choose the most logical answer.

I made a list of questions I didn't know the answer to. Questions like "Will my dad come home from work late today?" "Will I see so-and-so on the way to school today?" and "The next time I go grocery shopping with my mom, will we go to Store X?" filled my list. I took each question in turn and listened to the answer. The mind is a clever organ, and being tested made me nervous. Once I started the yes/no tests, my thoughts were more animated and quirky than ever. It became very difficult to calm my thoughts. Yes and no both seemed right.

At the time the apparent contradiction seemed like a major setback. My thoughts were a thick nest of distraction. How could I feel an answer if I couldn't even control my thoughts? Besides realizing I needed more practice learning to concentrate, I decided to read the question on the piece of paper and say out loud to myself, over and over again, "Yes yes yes yes yes yes yes yes," then "No no no no no no no no." Saying words out loud broke the silent distraction of my thoughts and helped me refocus on my testing. I repeated these words over and over and over and over in my head until one or the other "stuck." I realized yes and no also had a unique flavor or feeling to them, and depending on the question being asked aloud, one or the other flavor felt better to me. The process is extremely subjective, but eventually one answer feels stronger.

There was no science to my process. It was strictly based on feelings. I was trying to feel the feelings behind the words—emotionally and physically feel. Whenever I came up with the correct answer to a question, I noticed it had a very particular "feel" to it, much different from when I came up with the wrong answer. At first it was hard to zero in on which was which so I had to pay attention to the details. The first exercise in the chapter on increasing awareness was very helpful, because it helped me tune into the mechanical processes happening in my body. I learned how my thoughts affected me.

Correct intuitive answers "hook" in a way thoughts don't. Over time I discerned the "flavor" between the two information sources. My mental answers were always slower than my intuitive ones. Intuition always comes in a flash, with confidence, whereas my thoughts are a bit more wishy-washy. As my connection with my intuition increased, I started receiving answers to my questions before I'd finished reading them. I was strong enough to go back to visualizing the question internally. Sometimes I thought my question quietly within; sometimes I visualized a situation or person or feeling. Again, the process is very subjective, and you need to discover a particular method that resonates for you. Make sure you write your answers down next to your question. It's easy to forget what answer you came up with.

The flavor or character of your thoughts and intuitions changes over time. When I first started out, any time I'd get the right answer, my tongue tingled and my mouth salivated. It was inexplicable; it was simply what happened. Now I feel correct intuitive answers as a pressure on my sides coupled with a warmth in my navel. The concept of flavors is very fluid, just like your intuition. As the associations change, just have fun with it. It's one of the silly mysteries of being a psychic human.

Let's play the game and see what happens.

Exercise:
The Yes/No Game

Find a relaxing spot to practice and get comfortable. Earlier in the day may be easier at first, before the mind becomes too active. Bless the space you practice in, as we learned previously. When you are ready, make a list of questions with only a yes or a no as possible answers. Keep the questions simple. A question like "What will I have for lunch today?" or something similar will not help develop your intuitive skills. Open-ended questions have lots of possibilities. An example of a yes or no question is "Will my favorite daily special be on the menu at Subway today?" The first question cannot be answered with a yes or no. The second one can. (You can also look up the second answer on the Internet.) I also recommend questions about near-future events. Remember: you're trying to develop your intuition. Testing your skills is important. The more you test, the better you'll get. The only way to test more frequently is to wrap up your last list of test questions sooner than later. Only ask questions that can be answered within forty-eight hours. Otherwise developing your intuition takes too long.

Once you have your list of questions, go through the list and read the first question out loud. Stare at the question as you say the word Yes eight times in a row, then switch and say No. Keep going back and forth until one feels stronger than the other. As you get close to an answer, you can go back and forth between yes and no more quickly until you finally pick an answer. Use as much time as you need. I spend roughly one minute per question.

Next is the fun part. Since you've asked yourself a yes or no question about some future event, all that's left is to wait and see what happens. And really try to remember how your answer felt. Some people salivate when they get the answer. Others experience a particular smell. For some, experiencing the right answer feels like an itch in their brain. Some people suddenly, simply, calmly know what the answer is. However it comes to you, write down what you feel the answer is.

As each event transpires, refer to your list. Were you right or wrong? There can be no gray, no maybe or sort of. Reference your notes, mental or written. Correct answers are always your intuition. Wrong answers come from the mind's imagination. Learn to discern the correct flavor of the correct answer, and your intuitive accuracy will improve.

Much of the spiritual path aims to increase awareness, and the Yes/No game helps you increase awareness of the feeling and flavor of your intuition. Determining whether information comes from intuition or imagination is a matter of practice. Even though you may not hear your intuition correctly, and thus come up with a wrong answer to your question, the wisdom of your higher intuition is always right. Your imagination has a 50/50 shot at every question, right? If we want to learn to access our intuition clearly and effectively, then our job is to train ourselves to listen better. Eventually you learn the various flavors of your imagination and the regular flavor of your intuition. When you learn your personal flavors, you no longer need to do the exercise. You'll receive answers to questions before you can even form a complete sentence in your mind. Your feelings speak to your intuition, and through feelings you receive your answers.

The Influence of Calm vs. Attachment

At first, I was wrong a lot of the time because I hadn't become sensitive enough to tell the very subtle difference between my thoughts and my intuitive feelings. I was also very influenced by what I wanted the answers to be. Attachment to a particular answer was a major distraction. If attachment affects your ability to hear your intuition, ask only questions you're not attached to. Ask about mundane aspects of your life instead of questions about relationships or money. Ask simple questions about everyday life. Move on to the more difficult stuff later on. Make it easy to tune in to your intuition. Thirty years after first discovering my abilities, I still have a hit-or-miss connection to my intuition. I feel a solid intuitive connection with things pertaining to my own life but less so with others. Sometimes I'm spot-on, and sometimes I am totally off the mark.

I can't tell you how many times I've said, "I *knew* it. Why didn't I listen to my intuition?" Deep down we always know the answer. Remember to be gentle on yourself and try to remember to "feel" what the wrong answer felt like so you're not as confused next time. We are only humans, and we are fallible. The goal of the spiritual path is not to become godlike but to become completely, fully human. We are designed to be wise and benevolent creatures. The techniques in *The Way of the Psychic Heart* help you integrate your spiritual and everyday worlds together, but you'll still be a little human being in a very big world.

Eventually your intuition can become a very potent ally. Your general sense of timing and luck will increase because you'll be more tuned in to being at the right place at the right time. You'll have greater understanding of the issues afflicting people with whom you come in contact, which can help you become a more compassionate person. Following my intuitive guidance has led me on some amazing magical adventures and allowed me to be of service to other people in unique ways.

My first job out of college was working for an environmental cleanup lab. One Friday afternoon, as a deadline for a project approached, the department head in charge of the project came into my part of the lab asking if anyone had seen the project file. Someone had misplaced the file after its review process. To review a file, everyone who'd worked on the project double-checked their paperwork one last time. The file could have been anywhere.

While she searched frantically for the file, I *saw* the file she was looking for with an intuitive flash. The file was in a gray folder, not the manila ones we typically used, and I *saw* the file standing upright in a desktop file organizer. The file was in a dark room, but an open door allowed a little light to shine in on the desk and highlight the file organizer.

I kept having the same vision. I finally told the department head, and she looked stunned. I was describing her office, she said. Her lights were out, but her door was ajar. And she did have an upright file folder on her desk, but she had looked through it several times and the file she needed wasn't in there. When I asked her if the file folder was gray, her face paled.

She rushed off to her office and came back a few minutes later with the gray folder in hand. I was right. I saw the folder in a certain place but couldn't prove it was really there. And yet there it was. I had no way of knowing any details about her job, as I was working in a completely different part of the company. I was having a relaxed day, didn't care about the answer one way or the other, as the project didn't affect me in any way, and I was already friendly with my manager, so we had a connection established. These three things made it easier for me to tune in to her situation in a calm and relaxed manner.

Intuition is a tricky thing and works best when you're not attached to the answer, but you have to care enough about the answer to engage your intuition. Attachment is the biggest distraction to developing accurate intuition. Learning to pay attention without attachment is really a mind game. You have to want the truth more than you want a particular answer. Where the mind weighs and measures all options to come to the most logical or practical answer, intuition reaches the finish line in a flash. There is no reasoning, no method. You suddenly face your answer. Following your intuition is easier with practice, but the mind may regularly try to rationalize correct answers into wrong answers.

Intuition is also a skill you use differently at different times in your life. Developing intuition is a great help and comfort, a superior counselor and life guide. To live in tune with our intuition best aligns us with our life purpose. As we continue along our spiritual path, however, we become less grasping and more accepting of the flow of our life. We're happy with monotonous or dynamic life circumstances and learn to go with the flow. Living in alignment with our spiritual path puts us in a situation where, at the very moment we are most able to answer any question we want, we have no more questions and can take life as it comes.

My intuitive confidence has increased with my age, mostly because I've seen so many positive results from following my intuition in the past. This positive feedback has encouraged me to rely on my intuition no matter what when it comes to personal life decisions. If I'm asking my intuition about something happening in the world around me, I still get distracted or attached to a particular answer. Learning to develop your skills takes time and is affected by many things, just like every other skill we learn in life. When I was young and impatient, however, life gave me many opportunities to feel the difference between my thoughts and my intuition.

In college, I remember leaving a restaurant with gourmet takeout food from a specialty Tex-Mex place. I was impatient in college, and feelings of hunger only made it worse. I wanted to eat! I hopped in my little car with my takeout food and headed home. As I left the restaurant, a steady drizzle fell from the sky, and all my impatience and delicious imaginations about my upcoming meal dissolved. Everything stopped for a brief moment, and I had the distinct feeling that it was very important whether I turned left or right to go home.

Both ways led home, but I felt like I "should" turn right. As my stomach growled, my impatience flared. My brain began arguing about how each road was practically the same distance; there were probably more cops if I turned right because I'd be driving through the rich neighborhood; and other nonsense. In truth, turning left was just a little bit faster, and in my impatience I chose left.

I should have heard the heavens yell, "Prepare thyself, fool," but I wasn't listening. Traffic was slow but not horrible. I turned on some music and relaxed. There were delays along the way. I was stopped by several red lights and my impatience grew.

At one particular four-lane intersection, the light was green, but in the left lane an old brown Cadillac had stopped. Impatiently, I moved into the empty right lane and headed through the intersection at full tilt. A taxi slowly pushed its way through the intersection; hence the stopped Cadillac. But did I have any follow-up intuitions?

Of course!

My intuition was screaming at me to slow down. But did I listen? No.

Visibility was poor; the sun had set, and it was dark. The taxi and I entered the intersection at the exact same moment. Vehicles collided, and the force of impact pushed me off the road, with my front wheels smashing into an iron storm drain in the concrete curbing along the street. My front axle was demolished upon impact. I actually went airborne, careening between an old oak tree and a telephone pole, *clearing a hedge* before crash-landing in somebody's front yard.

We came down with a thud, the food and I, and the back axle crumpled. I slid toward a house until I made contact with it. Bricks from the corner of the old house rattled free and shattered the passenger window. It was a direct hit; the food was destroyed.

If I had gone right and taken the longer route, I would have missed the light by about three minutes, even with my impatient driving. Following my intuition would have kept me safe. The experience showed me the importance of paying attention to my intuition in the future.

Over the years you will perfect your form, learn your intuition's communication flavor, and develop your intuition into a reliable resource for information. Sometimes insights come in a flash and push through an otherwise distracted mind. Insights push to the forefront of our consciousness because they have an immediate bearing on our lives. Sometimes, hopefully all the time, you'll listen. The first step is to learn your style. The following exercise helps you gain more experience about what your style is.

Exercise:
Breaking through Distraction to Feel the Answer

Let's try getting answers without the technique of speaking "yes" and "no," and go directly to the source. The next exercise takes the game a step further. Now we'll try to hear a yes or a no right off the bat, loud and clear, immediately. Let's see if you can remain calm and simply know the answer to your most burning questions. You'll need a pad of paper, a pen or pencil, and a nice spot to curl up in.

Remember to keep your questions simple. Complex questions engage the mind and naturally tune out intuition. If you do have a complex question you want to answer, break the question down into smaller parts with a yes or no answer. Then put all the pieces together to gain a greater understanding about the more complex overall situation.

Let's try again.

As before, find a calm location to practice. Create a sacred space using the exercise Owning Your Space in chapter 1. Make yourself comfortable and take deep, complete breaths. Allow your mind to calm and relax. Say, "I am here in this space to practice developing my intuition. I honor my abilities and respect the fullness of who I am." Feel yourself in your body. Feel your energy field around you. Take a few moments and look at your aura. Tune in to how you feel and how strong your auric field is. Tell yourself you are going to ask yourself some questions and you'd like your intuition to tell you information about the questions. Ask for clear, concise answers.

When you are ready, write down your first yes or no question. As soon as the thought pops in your head, you may hear the answer. Either way, write down the first answer you hear, see, or sense. Feel the strength of the answer. Feel the flavor of the answer. Take a deep breath.

Continue until your questions have been answered. Did you feel a clear answer coming through? Was the flavor different this time?

With experience, answers naturally become more in-depth. The yes or no answer may be accompanied by visual or auditory information as well as physical responses. An example is asking questions involving another person and receiving intuitive information about a person outside the boundaries of your yes or no question. The information may be visual or auditory, or come to you in a flash like an old memory. Write down the information you received and try to verify the answer, just as before.

Whether you're able to verify the information or not, receiving more than a yes or a no as an answer is a sign your abilities are expanding. Remember to respect other people's boundaries and never randomly tune in to people around you without their permission. Invading someone's personal privacy is disrespectful and not in alignment with the qualities of a heart-centered life. There are times when random information is spontaneously received by you about people or things happening around you. Make sure your energy field is sealed up properly, or if you're still learning the sealing-up technique from chapter 4, quickly run through the exercise again. Skip the smudging part and move on to pulling your energy in and setting the intention to close any leaks or holes in your energy field. Really feel grounded in your body and fully present. Sealing up keeps you from randomly tuning in to people around you. Receiving random intuitions from the world around you is a sign your energy field is active without your awareness.

However, receiving additional information from your intuition shows that your abilities are getting stronger. Intuition can help you find out about anything. With the lost file, my intuition showed me a visual answer to the problem at hand. I didn't have to consciously ask a question. As the thought began to form in my head about where the file might be, the answer was already there.

When I receive intuitive guidance, I feel very calm. An answer comes to me so confidently that I feel there could be no other answer. But remember it takes time to get good at using your new skills. Be patient with yourself when you get something wrong; pay attention when you get an answer right; and be willing to try again. And always ask yourself yes/no questions until your skill level increases. Your intuition gives you the answer true for your situation. If there is no answer, perhaps the question doesn't pertain to what you are doing or the answer hasn't been decided yet. Perhaps you're asking something about the future involving other people and whatever they need to do hasn't happened yet. The free-will choice aspect to your question hasn't been chosen yet.

Trust Yourself

Whenever possible, I avoid using external tools to help develop psychic abilities. Many people use Tarot-type oracle cards, the I Ching, and other divinatory devices to help answer questions or see the future. I feel these things end up hindering people from learning to find the answers themselves. Oracles can be very helpful for those who haven't learned how to *see* yet, but as we walk our own spiritual path, these tools become unnecessary. In fact, once you feel your intuition is really strengthening, go back and do a reading with your favorite divination tool. Ask yourself whatever question you'd like and write down everything you receive as guidance from your intuition. Next, perform a Tarot or other divinatory card reading, pull runes, or do whatever other divinatory system you're comfortable with and compare the answers. How similar were the answers? Did you feel the oracle was correct? Which answer seemed most correct: your intuition or the oracle?

Oracle systems reflect what is happening inside us, from our thoughts to our feelings. Similar to any other divination tool, oracles are influenced by our thoughts, wills, hopes, and intentions for a particular answer, just like intuition. The mind can interfere in the divinatory process by creating expectations for a particular answer. Thankfully, if we've been practicing our intuitive development, we know the flavor of the mind. We can ignore the mind and focus on the flavor of our intuition. Oracle systems—through the actions of the way our bodies shuffle and choose the cards or rune or whatever— don't know the difference.

Oracles are influenced by whatever energy we're projecting the strongest. If we remain open and calm, our intuition will clearly influence the chosen oracle system to give the clearest and most accurate reading. However, our thoughts and fears will also influence the oracle if they are the strongest influence in that moment. Perhaps we fear a certain outcome or we're thinking really hard that we really want the cards or runes to say a particular thing. Those thoughts and emotions can easily outweigh the more gentle influence of our intuition. Only those who are very clear and calm can truly surrender their own desires to a higher influence and receive clear guidance from divinatory systems.

Quiz: Developing Intuition

Each month, quarter, or year, check in with your skill progression by self-assessing with the questions that follow. Developing your intuition is just like learning to ski or play poker or any other activity we learn in life. You're only competing against yourself. If you're studying *The Way of the Psychic Heart* with friends, you will soon discover you progress at different levels with different skills. Many skills even out over time. Some may not. Enjoy your personal progression and keep practicing. Opening up to your abilities is not a race or a contest. The following questions will help you assess your progress.

- How often do you engage your intuition in your daily life? Is intuition a helpful resource?

- How accurate are your answers? 50/50? 70/30? 100 percent?

- What subjects are the most difficult for you to get answers on? Remember to breathe and remain as calm and detached as possible to get the most clear and accurate answers.

- How much time do you spend tuning in to hear a correct answer? Have you noticed the time decreasing the longer you've practiced?

- What is the flavor of your thoughts? Pay close attention and remember the qualities of the flavor as a reference point. Be as descriptive as possible.

- What is the flavor of your intuition—meaning, what does the right answer feel like? Again, be as descriptive as possible.

- As you check back to these questions over time, how have your flavors changed?

- What do you like most about developing your intuition? How has intuition benefitted your everyday life?

- What do you want to achieve with your intuitive skills in the coming months?

Part III

Learning to Listen

Chapter Six

Dreams

Dreams are like stars ... you may never touch them,
but if you follow them, they will lead you to your destiny.
—ANONYMOUS

From now on, the skills we'll study are most successful if you have a basic proficiency in the skills from Part II. Continue practicing increasing awareness, seeing auras, and developing your intuition while you learn to develop these new skills. The more proficient you are with the skills from Part II, "Learning to See with the Three Pillars," the easier it will be to learn the rest of the exercises in the book.

In Part III, "Learning to Listen," we're going to learn how to listen to information already being shared with us in our dreams and by our spirit guides. Dreaming is something nearly everyone is already familiar with, so let's start there. Dreams are amazing mini-movies that keep us company at night. Some people believe they don't dream, though in truth they just don't remember. We all dream. Our dreaming life is just as rich as our waking life and deserves an equal amount of attention. We spend a lot of time sleeping, and a lot happens while we're peacefully curled up under the sheets. Parts of our consciousness subdued during the day awaken at night, including our higher self. Here in chapter 6 we'll look at the different types of dreams we experience and how dreamwork can help us on our spiritual path.

Human history is filled with epic tales with one or more plot twists involving dreams. Heroines and heroes dream of the gods and goddesses, of animals, of ancestors or recently departed loved ones—the possibilities are endless. Many fairy tales involve falling asleep and waking up in a different land, or being contacted in the dreamtime by someone from another world. Based on my experiences, these are not just literary devices to help move a story along. The dreams written into ancient myths were included because they actually happened. People today still have similar types of dreams. Like intuition, we can learn a lot about ourselves and the world around us by listening to dreams.

When we sleep, our waking mind calms down, but other parts of our consciousness remain awake. Whereas during the day we have to learn the flavor differences between our thoughts and our intuition, at night the mind poses less of a distraction. Our thoughts are still active but are more subdued. Quiet thoughts give space for physical, emotional, and spiritual dimensions of our consciousness to process and work through issues at night. The quality and richness of our dream life increases the longer we travel along our spiritual path. As our spiritual gifts unfold, our dream life becomes another psychic ability to work with.

Our waking consciousness lives within the box the mind creates. The mind's job is to create a cohesive external, three-dimensional experience for us, something we can rely on day after day. The mind teaches us how to live in the world by showing us what is real and what is not. The perception box in which we live is regularly modified and updated with new information. The mind adds repetitive elements and discards the rest. Prior to consciously activating our psychic abilities, the mind typically discards random and/or unique psychic experiences because such experiences are not a consistent part of our lives.

However, since the mind is such a flexible tool, as we walk the spiritual path and develop our psychic abilities, we have an opportunity to retrain it. The exercises in *The Way of the Psychic Heart* wake us up to a much larger world than our mind created for us. Each of us needs to teach our mind the world in which we wish to live. Dreaming is a safe bridge we can use to teach the mind to include more and more in its box of perception, because dreaming is an activity connecting what's inside the mental box of daily experiences to the part of us holding the box. Dreaming can become a bridge to help the mind yield its tight grip on our awareness to help open us up to our gifts, because dreaming is already something the mind considers normal and acceptable.

As you learn the basics of spiritual dreaming, be prepared to have some unique experiences. Strong psychic experiences occur in the dreamtime. These could take the form of direct messages from spirit guides, who communicate with us through the dreamtime just as easily as during our waking life. We may have dreams of the future and the past that shed light on key aspects of our personality and character or help us understand the connections we have with other people in our life, even seemingly minor connections. You may be contacted by deceased loved ones. Sometimes these ancestral contacts are only your mind processing loss but other times your ancestors are really communicating with you. Dreams have flavors, too, and you'll learn to tell different types of dreams apart.

Incorporating your spiritual life into your dreaming requires an open mind. Believing psychic experiences can occur while you dream is very important. Protect your personal space and set intentions before practicing in order to align yourself with experiences for your highest good and personal growth. We've already learned how to protect ourselves with the exercise Owning Your Space in chapter 1. Let's learn how to set intentions for our spiritual growth before going to bed.

Exercise:
Bedtime Intentions

Before retiring, create a list of intentions on a piece of paper you can read to yourself, quietly or aloud, each and every night. The list can be as long as you like but should include the following list of intentions. As you recite each intention, take a deep breath before moving on to the next one. Take the pause and be present to each statement. Feel the truth of the words and know all of these intentions will happen. Let your body, mind, and spirit absorb these intentions. Let them help you enliven your dream life.

1. *I will remember my dreams when I wake up in the morning.*
2. *I am open to meeting my spirit guides and other benevolent helpers in my dreams.*
3. *I release all tension from my day and clear my thoughts as I prepare to dream.*
4. *I know I am always protected in my dreams. I allow myself to relax completely while I sleep as my spirit guides protect me.*

For now we just want to set the stage for sleep, and tell the mind dreaming is normal. Also tell the mind to remember your dreams. Add any other positive suggestions you want to add to the list and repeat them, quietly or aloud, each night before bedtime. These intentions train your mind to pay attention to your dreams.

Dreaming is a very mysterious process. Many dreams seem to be as intricate and well produced as a blockbuster movie. There are characters, plots, subplots, unexpected twists and turns, deep revelations, and many breathtaking moments. But no matter how unexpected our dreams are, they are not random. Various types of dreams work in harmony while we sleep, each one yielding to the other as necessary for the betterment of our spiritual life. Therefore, respect your dream life. Dreams are a very personal experience, and anything you dream about has value. Try to understand what your dreams communicate.

To prepare for an active dream life, we will learn to sleep in a spiritual way. Be aware of how you think and feel before going to bed. Saying the affirmations listed on the previous page is a great way to make a clean break from any negativity, distraction, or chaos from the day and place yourself in a more calm, centered, and open state of being in which to dream.

Be aware of your sleeping situation, too. Embarking on the spiritual path is a lifelong process. Even though you'll still be a normal human being no matter how far you develop your spiritual life, once you start doing spiritual stuff you put yourself in a different space from your peers. You get used to having different types of experiences than you had before. Your higher self, spirit guides, and other benevolent beings know you want to grow and are present for your spiritual awakening.

Your personal development affects the spirit guides and higher self of the person you're sleeping next to. Seeing your interest in the spiritual, these beings may try to contact you through the dreamtime. Therefore, be sure you protect your personal space before going to sleep. Protecting your personal space ensures you have the most positive dreaming experiences and keeps you dreaming only about your own stuff and not someone else's.

Dreaming is a very important part of any spiritual practice. Let's talk more about the different types of dreams we experience at night. There are several types of dreams: some deal with mundane, everyday things, and some are more spiritually focused. I've broken them down into the following categories.

Processing Dreams

Processing dreams happen when your mind or emotions are trying to deal with something happening in your everyday life. Maybe you were too busy to reflect on the experience afterward, but your subconscious remembered. When you fall asleep, your higher consciousness goes to work digesting your waking experiences. Sometimes these processing dreams are replayed with various changes allowing you to feel empowered or embarrassed or confident or ashamed, depending on the situation. Life events are re-experienced positively or negatively depending on a lot of different personal psychological factors.

You know you're having a processing dream if you find yourself mortally embarrassed in your underwear at work, experiencing an amplified emotional replay of some recent traumatic experience, revisiting one of your favorite places, or if you dream someone you totally have a crush on is telling you how they actually have always liked you, too! These dreams are a way for us to digest poignant experiences in our lives, deal with our wildest fantasies, and otherwise process everyday life.

People who regularly meditate have fewer of these types of dreams. Even though we do not see the same images in our mind while we meditate, the same "digesting" process occurs. Meditation takes the highs and lows of daily life and moderates them by a process of consciously "digesting" these experiences while we meditate. Often, meditation surrenders all attachment to these experiences, thus releasing the negative charge of these experiences from our consciousness. Increasing awareness and developing intuition minimizes processing dreams because these skills bring understanding to what's really happening in daily life situations. We become less affected by negative experiences and can often see them in a positive light. Thus there are fewer negative life experiences needing to be digested. Many of the remaining experiences can be processed by meditation.

Processing dreams also occur from having an overactive mind. Some of us are more inclined to think than feel. An overactive mind prevents us from engaging in deep sleep and interferes with deeper levels of dreaming. We may sleep lightly, and our minds are still active. The cure is to wear out the restless part of our being. If we're fidgety, then we need to do something physically active. If we're mentally restless, we can meditate.

Overactive bodies are another cause of high frequencies of processing dreams. Unhealthy eating habits, including eating just prior to sleeping, keep the body agitated and active at night. An overactive body affects the mind and the dreamtime. The activity of the body keeps your mind active all night and your body relatively awake.

If you're the type who reads before falling asleep, or who is on the computer right up until you turn out the lights, you may be missing out on the other types of dreams. Many people who engage in excessive mental activity are not listening to their body trying to tell them to stop, calm down, and prepare for sleep. The mind can become attached to the constant stimulation provided by the twists and turns in the plot of a good book, or the endless amounts of information on a flickering screen. Some people think they need to overstimulate the mind in order to finally relax and shut it down for the night, and reading becomes a form of Ritalin. Eventually the act of concentrating and reading wears them out and they crash.

Reading until you crash may work, but it's not the best solution if your goal is to strengthen your dream life. Too much stimulation makes for restless sleep and excessive processing dreams. Many people who ignore their natural sleeping and waking cycles arise the next morning feeling very tired.

To minimize processing dreams, learn to meditate more. Meditation calms the mind and lets you gently face the issues of the day. A lot of the emotional and mental charge from these experiences is eliminated, resulting in a more peaceful, deep sleep.

Typically, if you have a hard time settling down, meditation can seem boring at first. There's a big difference between calm and boring. A hyper-stimulated mind has a narrow, laser-beam focus on just a few things. A calm mind is aware of much more but is not attached to these things as we are when we narrowly focus on one thing. When we're overstimulated, the brain is on massive overload and doesn't want to slow down. The mind wants to read or watch TV—anything to keep from being still and falling asleep. But becoming still is the one thing sure to help. Meditation is the best way to calm an overactive mind. It works better than reading, better than drinking warm milk, better than anything. Meditation brings you back to the present moment in a calm but complete way. Once you're fully here, relaxed, you can decide to fall asleep.

The other thing to do, as mentioned in chapter 2, "Spiritual Athletes," is to eat right. As a general rule, give yourself a couple of hours to digest your food before you fall asleep. If you're out late with friends having fun, don't worry about it. Let the dreamtime handle what's left to process from your day. But more often than not, try to let your body wind down before heading off to bed. A relaxed body benefits your dreaming life.

If you want more of the magical spiritual dreams, you'll need to free up some of the time currently taken up by the processing dreams.

For those of you who can't wind down at night, the following exercise should be done every night until your restless symptoms subside. Start with a fifteen-minute meditation, but keep increasing the time until you finally feel calm and can go to sleep. Once you are able to bring your consciousness back to the present moment and actually relax to the point of sleepiness, gradually reduce the time. Eventually you can skip the exercise, and simply telling yourself to sleep is enough to enter the dreamtime.

The following exercise is best done when you are ready to go to bed. Do the exercise in or near your bed. When you're done, turn out the lights and go to sleep.

Exercise:
Meditating

If you are new to meditating, set a timer nearby so you'll know when to stop. Start with fifteen minutes; adjust as necessary to achieve the desired effect.

Find a comfortable place to sit in your bedroom and make yourself comfortable. Sitting with legs crossed is ideal, but you can also sit in a chair. Use cushions to support your back or hips if necessary. Take a deep breath. Hold the breath as long as is comfortable. When you are ready to exhale, become aware of your body and relax. Imagine every muscle relaxing as you exhale, as we learned to do in the exercise Relax the Body in chapter 3.

Close your eyes. Take another long breath and hold it as long as you can. As you exhale, focus on your body. Feel yourself sitting in your bedroom. Take another long breath. Feel your body sitting still. Feel your muscles, bones, and joints supporting you. Take another breath. Feel your organs, your heart beating, your lungs breathing, your ears hearing, your nose smelling. Feel every organ you can as you meditate. Take another breath.

Continue allowing yourself to feel completely present as you sit and breathe. The more you pay attention to the breath, the more quiet your thoughts become. You may feel fidgety at first. This is normal. Simply continue breathing and allow your body to relax. The body responds to our thoughts. Calm thoughts provide space for the body to relax. Continue breathing. Take long, deep breaths.

Continue practicing for the time you've allotted and then go to bed. Continue breathing peacefully and let yourself drift off to sleep.

Meditation is extremely effective at helping us pause life and become centered. Deciding to stop for a few moments in time is a powerful act. You're exercising your power of choice. Choosing to meditate shifts your awareness from your brain's heightened activity back to your entire being. Become centered to process your waking experiences before you go to sleep for the night.

Symbolic Dreams

Symbolic dreaming happens when our higher self speaks to us in archetypal signs and symbols. If we can remember our dreams upon waking and write them down, then we can study their meaning later on. Symbolic dreams give us volumes of information about our life.

The types of symbols and archetypes we experience in our dreams have a lot to do with the culture we're from and the influences we take in during our waking hours, as well as the types of experiences giving us emotional highs and lows.

Kundalini is a Sanskrit word meaning "life force." In chapter 2, "Spiritual Athletes," we learned an exercise called Helping the Body Integrate Spiritual Energy, in which we moved energy up the spine and down the front of our body. The energy we moved was kundalini energy, and is often portrayed in ancient Indian literature as a coiled snake asleep at the base of the spine. After much practice, the kundalini energy thoroughly awakens, illustrated by ancient practitioners as a snake uncoiling up the spine. In many cultures, snakes were seen as positive and wise creatures. Uncoiling the kundalini force occurs on its own time once the process has begun. Attempts to force the kundalini to rise prematurely have a similar effect on the body as drugs do on the psychic doors of perception. The kundalini force takes time to work its magic on the body / mind / spirit, and much patience is required.

When my kundalini energy pathways were opening up, I had recurring dreams of rattlesnakes. I had a recurring dream I was sitting cross-legged somewhere out in Nature, peaceful and calm, when hundreds of pulsing rattlesnakes slithered up like bedsprings around my body. I felt the heat from their bodies as the snakes kept readjusting their positions when new snakes arrived. The snakes looked fierce but seemed perfectly content. There were hundreds of them piled up around me, each one curled up in a figure-eight position, head out front and tail poking out the back, to form a pyramid from the ground all the way up to my chin.

If that had happened while I was actually awake, I'd be screaming like a maniac for help. And I'd have processing dreams for years trying to deal with it. But during dreams, everything seems perfectly normal. The snakes' presence was reassuring and quite lovely. There was an audible hum/roar in the air with some fairy, tinkly, chimey sound mixed in. I felt a tremendous heat building up inside me and felt very, very strong. Snakes represent the kundalini life energy flowing through the body. So, to me, having a pyramid of snakes coiled up around me was a positive sign I was making progress in my practice. This dream is an example of a symbolic dream.

Providing us with personalized information is what symbolic dreams are all about. My higher self, the more mature and wiser aspect of my consciousness, spoke to me using visual images meaningful for me. Ultimately, it's best if you learn to interpret symbolic dreams on your own because nobody else knows you as well as you can know yourself. Consult books, websites, friends, and family to find out what other people think certain symbols mean if you'd like to, but always filter external perspectives against your intuition and decide what's true for you. My higher self spoke to me using symbols I personally found meaningful. I got the message and saw the whole experience as positive.

However, if you are the type of person who has a negative reaction to snakes, your subconscious knows this and responds accordingly. Someone shared a series of kundalini dreams with me that held a completely different symbolism. In the first few dreams there was a storm at sea, and she was barely keeping her head above water in the middle of the ocean. Over time the dream developed and changed. Suddenly a bright light shone inside her, and she was walking on the surface of the ocean during the same storm. She laughingly surfed a giant wave that rose up beneath her. For her the dream represented her body's dynamic life force (kundalini) integrating into her daily life (above water) and becoming the dominant perspective. Instead of floating in the water getting pulled along by the random currents of life, the light of her kundalini power awoke.

One way our higher selves communicate with us is by giving us information in a way we can best understand with a minimum of effort. Write down your dreams to help you see patterns of repeating information.

Symbolic messages include anything meaningful to you. Meaning can be found in numbers, shapes, geographical images such as mountains or oceans, important people or mythical persons we're familiar with—anything, really.

Interpretation

There are many wonderful books about dream symbols and their meanings, but ultimately your dreams are personal experiences especially designed for you by your higher self. Each of us needs to find our own meaning from our own experiences. Reference books are very helpful, but over time these always take a backseat to your own perspective. With enough experience from many years of practicing, you will understand the meaning of your dreams. Meaning comes as a certainty derived from having a strong intuition. Every practice builds on what came before, so be sure to continue working on honing your intuition while learning the dream exercises.

"We only receive what we can handle." This spiritual aphorism has helped me through many a stressful situation. And just as my life experiences have been doled out to me in manageable doses, so too is the information shared with us by our higher selves. As we grow and change through life, our dreams change, too. As our spiritual life expands and deepens, our dreams become richer and more meaningful. You may dream of a generic animal, such as a horse. As your spiritual practice deepens and you are more connected with your higher self, you may find yourself having a meeting with the "Goddess of All Horses" with a special message or task for you to complete. These experiences are amazing and are often the start of unique transformational periods in our lives. Spiritual and psychic dreams blow regular dreams out of the water.

As always, finding the willingness and curiosity to learn more about ourselves and our human spiritual potential feeds a rich and rewarding inner life. Write all of your symbolic dreams down in your journal. The mind learns to remember dreams when you take the time to write everything down. Keeping a journal encourages us to have even more deep and meaningful dreams. Certain dreams are seasonal; others occur after hanging out with certain friends or loved ones; while others are triggered by experiences at a job. Finding patterns helps you decipher the messages contained in your dreams and helps you learn more about what's influencing you in your everyday life.

Exercise:
The Dream Journal

Write down your dreams upon waking each and every morning, seven days a week. If you're rushed for time, take five minutes and write down the main details of the dream. What was the plot? Who were the main characters? Describe the scenery and the sights, smells, sounds, and feelings present during the dream so you can come back later and fill in the details.

Include the date and time in your journal each day you write. Associating a dream with a particular day and time grounds the experience in the daily world. The mind is more likely to remember something associated with a "normal" part of your everyday life. Date your dreams to remember your dreams with a clarity and detail not previously experienced.

Taking the time to write down your dreams day after day, week after week, helps you find patterns. Notice how the stories in your dreams change as you learn from their messages. Notice their deepening clarity and meaning. And notice how your dream images become so much clearer as you gain experience seeing energy and following your intuition.

Dreaming of the Future

My great-grandmother often dreamt of things to come and told her children and grandchildren about them. She dreamt about my parents' divorce before it happened. She dreamt about our dog's death shortly before he died. She even dreamt of her own death a few months before her passing. She remained open to these experiences throughout her life. She had a natural talent for dreaming of the future, or *precognitive dreaming*.

Precognitive dreaming, along with its twin, dreaming of the past, may spontaneously occur as you continue on your path of spiritual awakening. Some people interpret symbols in dreams and apply them loosely to future events, which is not the same thing as having a precognitive dream. Those are symbolic dreams, as I've described. The kinds of dreams I'm talking about here are dreams in which you dream about an actual event, write the experience down in your journal, and then the dream comes to pass in the future. You can reference your dream journal to see how closely your dream was to the future reality. When a precognitive dream unfolds in reality, small details commonly change, such as the type of clothes you're wearing or the color and type of objects appearing in the dream. This is normal.

These dreams have always been spontaneous for me, and typically occurred at times in my life when major life changes were afoot. In the years before and after my parents' divorce when I was in high school, I often dreamt of the future. Many of those dreams were seemingly random, and at the time I had no idea why I was dreaming about such random things.

In one dream, which took place during the winter, I was walking to school by an old Victorian house. I approached a large crack in the sidewalk, and a gigantic mass of ants were swarming over the crack, creating a new home. I wrote the dream down. Time passed. The following spring I walked to school as usual, passing by the same Victorian house as usual with my friends, when I stopped dead in my tracks. The ant swarm was there. I stared at it from the same angle as I had seen it in the dream. Nothing else out of the ordinary happened during the rest of the day.

The real-life reenactment of the dream happened a few months before my parents' divorce, and I saw the dream as a marker around a significant period in my life.

"How come if you're so psychic you didn't dream of the actual divorce?" I often asked myself. Perhaps you thought it, too. The answer is, "I have no idea."

As I mentioned before, being open to your spiritual gifts doesn't give you omnipotence, just as learning to speak doesn't mean you can automatically speak every word in every language. And the ability to remember doesn't imply an absolutely impeccable knack to recall every life event down to the most boring detail.

Sometimes we have nonlinear experiences and our intuition is a wonderful guide to help us sort our experiences into meaningful events. In this case, my intuition told me these premonitions were happening around emotionally traumatic events in my life.

I had another dream in which a woman came to talk to me at my job. There was nothing particularly memorable about her, but I couldn't stop staring at her. I zeroed in on her face. It seemed really important to remember her. I woke up the next morning and wrote down the seemingly random, meaningless dream. Soon I forgot the whole thing. Time passed. I worked extra hours during summer break from school. One day the girl from the dream came in to my work. She had the same clothes, hair, look in her eyes, everything. There was a major difference, however: we never said a word to each other.

Remember when I mentioned that testing is an important part of the spiritual path? Testing is especially important when dreaming of the future. It doesn't do you any good to say you've had a precognitive dream when there is no evidence the dream ever mirrored a real-life event. To say otherwise is only feeding your imagination. Until you actually can prove to yourself that what you dreamt actually happened, keep your eyes and ears open. Hold the intention you are willing to be in the right place at the right time to see a dream unfold in the real world. Gain the confidence to discern the "flavor" of a precognitive dream of the future versus a processing or symbolic dream.

Being able to merge your spiritual life with the everyday, ordinary world ensures you are indeed having psychic experiences and are not going insane.

Guide Dreams

The final type of basic dreaming I'd like to mention is the *guide dream*. Guide dreams are very special. Guide dreams are a way for our spirit guides to directly communicate with us. Similar in flavor to dreams of the future or past, guide dreams have a very different feel from a processing or a symbolic dream. In these dreams you are visited by actual spirits. Guide dreams are not figments of your imagination. Some spirits who visit you have visited other people as well, and you can compare your notes to theirs to find the similarities.

I had a significant guide dream when I was twenty-one. I woke up in a lucid dream, which is a state of consciousness where you are awake mentally but physically your body is still sleeping. Some people have a very distinct sensation of their body lying asleep in bed as their dreaming body runs around in the dreamtime. Lucid dreams have a heightened sense of reality compared to processing dreams. You feel wind on your face if you're outside; you taste food, feel the grip of a handshake, and experience things in a lucid dream as you do when awake.

The dream began in a desert in India. I stood on the edge of a dried-up riverbed. The wind was strong, and the sky was a rich, lively blue. The sun was bright in the sky overhead and I could feel its rays warming me. Everything had a sound: the sky hummed; the drops of sunlight vibrated; the wind sang.

Suddenly a trumpet blared, and I turned to look up the dry riverbed to the source of the sound. A group of snow-white-and-gold angels hovered above and around a litter carried by women and men dressed also in white and gold. Several held parasol-type umbrellas with little dangly bon-bons. The procession made its way slowly downriver toward me and stopped.

Two angels approached the litter and helped a young woman make her way to the edge of the dusty riverbank. She came over to me smiling, and we meditated. She kept chanting, "Mudra Meera, Mudra Meera," over and over and over while making specific hand gestures. She taught me a few things that particularly applied to my spiritual path, and then I woke up. The experience was intense. Every flavor of real life occurred in the dream: I felt the wind on my face, smelled desert life on the warm air, heard sounds all around my body, and felt my body present in the dream as if I was really there.

Prior to this dream I'd never been attracted to Eastern philosophy or religion. I loved Native American, Egyptian, Middle Eastern, and European history. But the experience inspired me to study Asian history, mysticism, and cultures.

Upon waking the next morning, I began researching the dream. The phrase *Mudra Meera* led me to Mother Meera, and a book about a young woman known by the same name written by Andrew Harvey. There were several pictures of her in his book. One in particular was a photo of her from her late teens. She looked *exactly* like the woman in my dream. I was dumbfounded. One of the most striking things about her in my dream was the intensity in her eyes. Her eyes peered deeply into my heart. I later learned many other people had been dreaming of her in their own way.

As with precognitive dreams, guide dreams are usually beyond our control. There are many shamanic paths throughout the world that include lucid dreaming as an integral part of their practice. However, many of these traditions have the practitioner actively seek out contact with higher spiritual beings of one form or another. There are very specific rituals and practices designed to lead the practitioner to increasingly engaging experiences with these other forms of life. Active dreaming taken to such a high level is best done under the direct guidance of an experienced teacher.

The more you write your dreams down, the more dreams you will have. Paying attention to dreams feeds the dreaming process. The business saying "What gets attention, gets done" applies to everything in life, including your dreams. If you pay attention to your dreams, then your dreams will increase. It's just that simple.

If dreaming isn't your thing or you have unpleasant, intense dreams, remember you are in control of your experience. Ask your higher self to turn off your dreaming abilities until you are ready to practice again. The psychic development practices in *The Way of the Psychic Heart* work together to help you have a more engaged, happy, and productive daily life. Start with what's comfortable while remaining open to the possibilities of future growth.

Chapter Seven

Automatic Writing

This is a course in miracles—please take notes.
—MESSAGE RECEIVED BY HELEN SCHUCMAN

Helen Schucman was a professor of medical psychology at Columbia University from the late 1950s to the mid-1970s. Helen heard the above-quoted sentence in the early 1960s, and from 1965 to 1972 she wrote down everything she heard. Through these series of automatic-writing experiences, she produced *A Course in Miracles*, which was first published in 1976. In this chapter we'll explore the concept of automatic writing and do exercises designed to help you experience automatic writing for yourself.

What Is Automatic Writing?

Automatic writing is the process of writing down information heard, felt, remembered, or otherwise received by our intuition, spirit guides, or other nonphysical sources. Automatic writing is a more advanced form of the simple Yes/No exercise featured in chapter 5, "Honing Intuition." As your intuitive sense gets stronger, automatic writing should be easy to do. In fact, automatic writing can spontaneously occur.

Automatic writing is a simple process: you write down questions and listen for the answer. There is a difference between automatic writing and asking your intuition questions. With automatic writing you set the intention to access more than intuition. The questions can be anything at all, and can often spontaneously take the form of a conversation between you and the source of the information. Remain mindful of the character of the sources of information you're communicating with. Each one is unique and has its own flavor association, just as we learned about with our thoughts and intuition.

Automatic writing connects you with new flavors of information. These sources of information include your spirit guides communicating with you, your ancestors, or even other types of spirits, such as Nature spirits. As your intuition continues opening, remember to seal up and set the tone for the practice by blessing your personal space and staying as alert as possible during the process of automatic writing. Refer to chapter 1 for a refresher on these exercises. Bless your space to ensure nothing negative comes through in the writing.

Let's go through the basic automatic-writing exercise together and see what happens.

Exercise:
Automatic Writing

As usual, find a comfortable place to relax. Choose a place where you can remain comfortable throughout the entire exercise and stay focused on your experience. Bring a journal and pen to write with. Perform the Heart Smudging exercise as described in chapter 1. When you are finished, find a relaxing place to practice automatic writing and say the following blessing:

"To all my spirit guides who work for my highest good, please join me now as I practice automatic writing. If anyone other than my guides wants to talk to me through automatic writing, you have to go through my guides first, who make sure you are of high quality and determine if communicating with you is for my highest good. Thank you for being a resource on my spiritual path."

As usual, take several long, slow, deep breaths to calm your mind and body and become fully present to what's happening. Let yourself be relaxed yet very aware and present to where you are in your room and the way your body feels. Be present yet relaxed. Choose a theme for your automatic-writing session, such as your job, your love life, or your health. Only after doing the blessing, setting the intention, and becoming centered do we write down the questions. Make a list of questions, leaving enough space between them to write a few paragraphs of material.

Ask questions from the heart. What's bothering you? What would you like to know about the next phase of your life, career, or relationships? Think of automatic writing as connecting with your own psychic hotline.

There are two ways to experience how automatic writing feels different from regular writing. The first way is to read your question quietly or out loud and then look away as you let your hand write the answer. Involuntary body movements may feel weird at first. Write one question at a time because you'll most likely write much larger than normal and scribble all over the page. When you are finished, look at your answer. If you're satisfied with the answer, move on to the next question. If not, write some follow-ups and repeat the process of reading the question to yourself or aloud and then looking away as your hand writes.

With practice you can hear or see anyone talking to you as you write, using abilities to see energy and tap into your intuition learned in Part II, "Learning to See with the Three Pillars." How does the writing feel? Is it masculine or feminine? An outside force moves your hand, and if I were you, I'd be curious to know more about that force. With practice you become more adept at writing down your answers and receiving very clear answers right away, without the need for as many follow-up questions.

As you become more familiar with the force guiding your hand, there is a very good chance you will hear or feel or see the force guiding your hand as the words are scribbled down on the page. However, if the idea of something else working your hand other than you does not appeal to you, then try the second option, which is just below. In truth, I only use the second option.

The second way to do automatic writing is to write down what you hear as you think or say each question. The process is similar to having a conversation with yourself, but the voice or voices talking to you don't sound like your own voice. Your own internal voice has a certain tone and feel missing from the conversations you have during automatic-writing sessions. You are learning to actually communicate with forms of consciousness without physical bodies but present in your life nonetheless.

Write down whatever you hear, feel, visualize, or otherwise experience as the answer, then ask any follow-up questions. Write down any other questions you have. Many times, as soon as you think your next question, the answer arrives. Receiving quick answers means your intuition communication skills are working. Your intuition processes information much faster than the brain, and therefore seemingly spontaneous answers are the norm rather than the exception.

No matter how fast the answers come to you, take the time to write down your questions and their answers. A true message from your guides is consistent, so if you need to re-ask the question, the answer should be exactly the same no matter how much time passes.

If at any time you feel confused about what the automatic-writing experience is telling you or you get tripped up on a particularly garbled word, then, from my experience, such an occurrence indicates the mind is interfering in the process. A normal function of the mind is to replay events, even those that occurred only a moment prior. Replaying events is one way the brain continuously creates the "reality box" within which we live.

If the brain's activity becomes a distraction, stop the exercise for a moment and collect yourself. Take a few calming breaths and allow your mind to clear. Even though the mind continues to replay events in the background, with your attention bring your primary focus back to the exercise. Feel yourself in your space, feel the spirit guide or guides around you, and, when you're ready, try again. Next time, attempt to feel the flavor and sound of your own internal dialogue versus the voices of your guides. With practice you can sense your own thoughts and gently ignore them, choosing instead to focus on the voices of your guides. Over time your confidence will grow, and you will learn to ignore your own mental chatter.

When you are finished with your automatic-writing session, thank everyone who showed up to assist you and say goodbye for now. Put everything away, seal up your energy *field as learned in the exercise Sealing Up, Version One in chapter 4, and go about your day.*

I like automatic writing when I'm looking for a perspective outside myself. If I'm still not sure of the difference between my thoughts and intuition, or if I'm feeling too agitated to get a clear answer, then I'll ask the same questions through automatic writing. Through the years, automatic writing has helped me to deepen my sense of the "flavor" difference between my thoughts and my intuition, and to reconnect with my spirit guides. The answers you receive can be very detailed, even if you asked a general question.

In my late twenties, I had an extremely specific automatic-writing session. I'm sharing it with you to show you just how detailed the information from an automatic-writing session can be.

I was in between relationships, and the question "I wonder what my next girlfriend will be like?" popped into my head. I didn't feel a strong connection to my intuition about the answer because I probably had a lot of expectations about who the person might be. My mind kept firing off question after question: What will she look like? How old will she be? My mind's grasping became a distraction, and I couldn't hear my intuition.

I grabbed a pen and paper and wrote down the question. I could feel my guides' sense of humor before I even got the question out on paper. I was told I'd meet her in two weeks;

she'd be 5' 8" with blond hair and blue eyes; and she'd be a writer. The information was pretty specific. As I received information, I also felt some of the "flavor" of the woman they described to me. My guides went on to tell me specific details about the relationship, her beliefs, and other personal information. My guides even told me how long the relationship would last if situation A occurred, and how much longer if situation B happened. If we started dating, there were choices to be made between us affecting the future, and since those choices hadn't yet been made, the future was still in motion.

In the manner of the section "Recalling Spiritual Events" from chapter 1, once the mini-reading was done, I completely forgot about it. I went to work, hung out with friends, and carried on with my life. Even though during the automatic-writing process I was amazed at the information I received, if I hadn't written anything down, I might have forgotten the details forever.

Two weeks passed, and my friends invited me out dancing. Swing dancing was all the rage back then, and a bunch of us practiced together every week. I arrived at the club and walked downstairs where we always met up. I looked around for my friends, but apparently I was the first one there.

I wandered the crowd while I waited. All of a sudden something hit me like a brick. I felt very centered and aware of my surroundings. I felt my guides surround me. I felt a pressure on my cheeks as one of my guides literally held my head in what felt like a pair of hands. I felt them gently turn my head to look toward a far corner of the club. A light shone across the dance floor like a spotlight onto a young woman's face on the other side of the dance floor. Several spirit voices simultaneously said, "That's her. She's the one we told you about."

Needless to say, I was shocked. The memories of the automatic-writing session came back in a flash. I figured if it was meant to be for me to date her, then there was nothing to worry about. If I asked her out, she had to say yes, right? I walked right up and started talking to her. She had blond hair and blue eyes, was 5' 8", and amazingly she was also a writer.

My guides, through the process of automatic writing, told me about a future event that actually happened. As I got to know her, every detail about her personality and beliefs received from my guides was true as well. I had never seen her before in my life. Even if I had subconsciously started looking for a blond-haired, blue-eyed woman who was 5' 8" tall, what are the odds she'd be a writer?

The Importance of Being Prepared

If you asked questions about something specific, then you should attempt to discover whether or not the writing session turned out to be true. If the session provided you with accurate information, then you successfully tuned in to either your intuition or your guides. If the information turned out to be bogus, then your mind interfered or perhaps you were led astray by a mischievous spirit. If you seal up properly, have practiced sealing up your energy field regularly before going out into the world, and if you practice saying your affirmations regularly, owning your space, increasing awareness, and everything else described between the beginning of the book and now, then the likelihood of random influences interfering with your automatic writing is very, very low, and chances are your mind got in the way of your spiritual clarity.

If you haven't been practicing, however, then you may not be prepared to open yourself as wide as is needed to communicate via automatic writing. A lack of preparedness causes unnecessary problems as you attempt to open up and develop your psychic abilities. Once you have experiences and connect with the spiritual part of your life, respect the process of spiritual awakening enough to act responsibly and not try things before you're ready.

As mentioned previously, your spiritual experiences should help you become a more integrated and capable member of society. Your experiences give you the strength to face life challenges, find solutions to problems, understand your inner workings, and have compassion for problems other people face in their lives. If at any time your experiences are in opposition to these perspectives, then something is not proceeding correctly, and I advise you to seek professional assistance.

Automatic Writing vs. Mental Illness

What's the difference between hearing the voices of spirit guides or our higher self and the mental illness schizophrenia? I mean, there's always the potential I just made up an entire dialogue between different, fractured parts of my mind, right? What if I made the whole thing up and had a conversation with myself, perhaps the first step down the road to a severe mental illness?

Well . . . all I can say is, my own automatic-writing sessions have shown me information about real-life situations so many times that I'm convinced my experiences have nothing to do with my imagination. I have enough history as a productive citizen to be satisfied I am psychic and not mentally ill. I built up a multimillion-dollar business from scratch, helped save over a thousand acres of land from development by working with local government and nonprofits, and have otherwise proven I am a fully functional member of society.

Living with psychic abilities gives you a different way of seeing the world. I feel, see, and hear spirits talking to me whenever I choose to focus on them because they literally fill the world from top to bottom. Spirits of all kinds are everywhere: in the city and the country, in my house and at my job, around my family and friends as well as pets and wild animals. Earth is full of spirits.

When I first began my spiritual awakening, I was young and didn't have people around me to talk to about these sorts of things. I experienced much self-doubt, but every cloud has a silver lining. To ensure I wasn't going crazy, I sought out ways to use my psychic abilities to learn more about the everyday world. I specifically asked questions of my guides I couldn't know the answers to and then tested those answers against what happened in daily life. When I truly tuned in to either my intuition or my guides, the information received was correct.

My experiences have enhanced my everyday life and my relationships with others. My abilities have helped me integrate into the world instead of retreating. I experience the world in ways that seem magical to those who've yet to open to their abilities. Intuitive and spiritual guidance has given me insight into the "whys" and "hows" of the world. Because of these insights, I have hope that humanity isn't hurtling headlong toward disaster.

Those whose spiritual path compels them to hide from life, whether from a cult influence or a real psychosis like schizophrenia, are in dire need of help. With your spiritual practice, if learning to hear voices leads you to withdraw from the world, then something unhealthy is happening with your spiritual practice. If you feel you want to do harmful things to yourself or other living things in the world around you, something unhealthy is going on. You may be having a bad day, feeling a mild case of escapism, or it could be something more serious. If you have any questions about what is happening during your sessions, I recommend discussing your experiences with a professional therapist, in particular one who is open to and understands psychic phenomena. Learning to open to your psychic abilities is designed to help you be more *in* the world. Seek help immediately if you are having a different result.

Protecting and blessing your personal space keeps a positive, healing vibration around your spiritual exercise. Places in which you meditate and practice spiritual exercises should feel light and happy and free compared to the rest of your home. Take this seriously, as we live in a much larger world than our brains like to acknowledge and not everything is friendly to humans. I share the worldview of many traditional societies that see everything around us as alive and capable of interacting with us in some form or another. By practicing techniques to interact with the large, complex world of spirit, you are agreeing to live by its rules whether you realize it or not. Therefore, treat these practices with respect and proceed in a steady, step-by-step fashion. Remember the sequence of exercises is designed to progressively open you to your psychic gifts while keeping you safe at the same time.

So enjoy your practice, protect your personal space, and honor the power you are developing within yourself. I personally have never met anyone or worked with anyone who developed a mental disorder from engaging in spiritual practices; I only mention the possibility so you have all the information available to you as you move along your path.

In the next chapter, we'll look at the subject of spirit guides more in-depth. Eventually, you will not need to use automatic writing in order to communicate with your spiritual family. The doors of spirit will be open enough to allow open, free dialogue without pen and paper.

Chapter Eight

Spirit Guides

We are all guided by spiritual teachers
who speak to us in our dreams.
—BARBARA ANN BRENNAN

What Are Spirit Guides?

Automatic writing is a great segue into the subject of spirit guides. Guides guide us, and spirit guides do the same thing. As we walk through life as human beings, a group of spiritual beings assigned especially to us help us as we live our lives. Spirit guides are ever-present forms of spirit and light, and have agreed to hang out with us from birth to death. Guides are not allowed to interfere in our growth, choices, personal interactions, or other earthly decisions unless we specifically ask them for help. Think of them as a fan club comprised of the most supportive and positive guardian angels you could think of.

Guides come in all shapes and sizes and originate from many sources. Some are very ancient; some are ancestors from your bloodline who have agreed to watch over future generations. Having guides near as you walk through life may sound a bit awkward, but in truth these beings are very respectful of your personal space. Guides are always concerned for our safety, health, and well-being, but as I mentioned, they do not interfere with our daily lives unless asked.

Your guides become super-excited you've embarked on your path of spiritual awakening. Guides have a lot to tell you and can be a wee bit overzealous to get their message out at first, but you are always in control of your personal space. Spiritual law says when you own your space, everything in the world has to respect your space. You set the tone about what influences enter your sphere of awareness. If you've been practicing protecting your personal space, then you should be fine. Many spiritual traditions talk about how, once you've embarked upon your spiritual path, random events no longer happen to you. Everything in the multifaceted world around you conspires to bring only those events into your life to help you learn your life lessons and grow as a soul. As long as you continue to walk the spiritual path, these conditions remain in place.

If you haven't continuously practiced protecting and owning your personal space, hear me when I say that you need to if you want to have the most positive results later on. As we get into the parts about actually interacting with things living in the heretofore invisible side of life, it is *extremely* important to own your space. Protecting your personal space sends a clear message you respect your energy field and your life and lets your guides and other spirits know they must connect with you on your terms, not theirs. The same rules apply in daily life; if you own your space, you gain the respect of your peers.

Anytime that guides agree to help a human out in life, both the human and the group of guides agree to do so. Neither side is forced into a situation. At the same time, the experience was meant to happen and was most likely orchestrated through events set in motion long ago. There's nothing random in life. Everything in the universe is conspiring to help you wake up and grow. We're all like little seeds and need to self-water in order to grow. The guides are here to help us remember where the watering cans are and how to use them, so to speak.

Sometimes our guides warn us of impending doom. Some offer guidance about particular things happening or about to happen in our life. Some help us remember how connected we all really are to each other. Others keep harmful influences away from us. But most are simply present with us on our journey.

Simply introduce yourself to your guides and let them know you're open to talking to them, seeing them, or otherwise interacting with them. The following exercise is a simple way to meet your guides.

Exercise:
Meeting Your Guides

As always, create sacred space using the exercises detailed in chapter 1. Next, take several long, deep breaths to calm down and become fully present to what you are doing. Become aware of the space around you, your body sitting comfortably, and any sounds around you, as learned in chapter 3. Take several more deep breaths.

Become aware of your energy field. Feel the different layers of your body, from your internal organs and bones out to your muscles and skin. Then feel the layers of your aura extending from your skin out into the space around you. Continue breathing, inhaling not just the air but the energy in the air, too. As you exhale, feel the breath move through your energy field. Notice how the breath and your energy field interact. Feel how layers of energy touch your auric field and extend into the world around you.

Say quietly or aloud, "I am here today to meet my guides. I only allow in the highest-vibration guides to enter my personal space. If you want to introduce yourself to me, do so now." Let yourself be open to the possibility of meeting your guides. Different guides have different energies, and some have a density similar to one or more layers of your energy field. If you can sense your aura, you can sense your guides.

You'll find most psychic impressions have their own flavor. We've learned about flavors with many other skills, and so it is with our guides. Take several slower, deep breaths but maintain your awareness of everything happening around you. Observe any changes in your energy field. Do you feel any other presences around you? Do you hear, smell, taste, feel, or see any new flavors around you with any of your psychic senses, whether as internal visions and sounds or externally? If so, where are these sensations located? Behind you, supporting you, or in front of you, greeting you face on? Overhead or off to the side? Wherever you have a sensation is fine.

Some people feel a warm, loving presence around them; some feel nebulous, angelic lovingness to comfort them. Others feel specific relatives show up, which can be emotionally bittersweet. Maintain a connection if you wish; otherwise stop the interaction at any time. There is nothing to fear. You are completely safe in your personal space. At any time you can command any spirit in your presence to leave your personal space immediately. Seal up your energy field and bless or smudge your house for good measure to complete the disconnection process. Be completely present no matter what happens. And, of course, if you are enjoying the experience, continue interacting with whomever arrives to speak with you until you are ready to stop.

You may not experience dramatic contact. You may only notice your body's reaction to the experience, such as warmth in the heart or a feeling of relaxation and peace. With practice you can develop your ability to see to the point where you actually do visually see your spirit guides and hear their voices.

Sometimes people can have a very intense first experience, especially when the experience involves a passed relative or loved one. No matter how much you believe in the possibility of psychically contacting your guides, first contact can be a real shock to the system. No matter what happens, even if you don't sense anything happening, know you have made contact. Your intention shapes your life; if you intend to meet your guides, then you will meet them. Our reality follows our intentions and shapes how we experience the world around us.

When you are ready to finish your session, say to yourself or aloud, "Thank you so much for introducing yourself to me. I appreciate your presence and attention. I have to go now, but I will return when I am comfortable for more contact."

If you are open to regular contact, you can also say:

"I have to go now, but please stay with me as I walk through life and feel free to give me guidance as necessary."

Come back to the everyday world. Stand up, stretch, move around until you feel completely grounded and present. Seal your energy field up by pulling your energy into your body as we learned previously. Visualize all energetic contact with the world being disconnected and all of your energy back in your own field. Tell yourself you are whole and complete and fully present.

Write down any experiences you had during your session in your journal, as well as details about the nature and personality of any guide you encountered. Be sure to write down any messages received from your guides. Guides are a unique resource. The more you listen to your guides, the more they have to say. But always remember they are present to help, not overwhelm, you. If at any time the experience becomes too intense, simply tell your guides to give you some space and they will.

I have a deep love for Nature. I discovered my passion in high school, and it was one of the reasons I decided to study environmental science in college. As I mentioned early in this book, my family owned a large piece of land left wild for over a hundred years that we called "The Property." It is now part of an even larger preserve, but back in high school the land was still in our family. Towering trees, wildflower meadows, swamps, kettle lakes, and streams shelter many different types of habitats and hundreds of different species of plants and animals.

One day during my senior year of high school, I drove out to the Property to have a look around. After a while I wanted to rest. I let my intuition guide me to a large, old aspen with a bent top. As I looked up to the top of the tree, I noticed the biggest, fattest raccoon I've ever seen sleeping up there in the bend in the tree. The raccoon's fur drooped over the edge of the aspen trunk.

I saw its fur gently rise and fall and felt comfortable it was asleep. Yes, I knew raccoons have a reputation for being aggressive, but I felt guided to sit under the tree and rest, so I did.

I looked around and saw the most unusual-looking group of plants. I later discovered the plants were downy rattlesnake orchids. I had no idea orchids even grew in places that experienced harsh winters; I'd only heard of them growing in tropical areas. I was shocked to realize no one in my family had ever seen these plants, even though we'd had the land for twenty years. I decided to try and learn every plant on the Property.

As my psychic abilities matured and I became more comfortable interacting with spiritual beings on a regular basis, I spent more and more time at the Property. The land was full of spirits of all kinds, and as we got to know each other, they helped me discover new plants on a regular basis. Guides woke me up in the morning to tell me a new plant was ready to meet me at the Property.

I'd drive to the Property, excited for what was in store for me. My guides were excited, too, and were always with me each step of the way. I'd walk to the edge of the land near where I parked my car and think to the spirits of the land, "I'm here. Where do I go next?"

Remember how my guides held my head and showed me the woman at the dance club? Well, it was a similar experience in the forests of my family's land, except I felt a pull in my chest to move in a particular direction. If I was unsure or didn't feel a pull, I asked, "Straight, left, right, or back?" in a manner similar to the Yes/No exercise aimed at building intuitive skills. The spirits of the land pulled me in a particular direction, and off I followed.

I was led everywhere. The spirits took me the shortest distance between where I was standing and where the new plants were growing. Every time I listened to their call, I was rewarded with a new plant discovery. I ended up finding several other species of orchids, gentians, and other rare and protected plants as a direct result of their guidance.

Each of us has an affinity for certain spirits and guides. I have always loved Nature, and I'm not surprised I've had so many cool adventures in Nature as a result of my partnership with Nature spirits as some of my spirit guides. These guides have been in the form of ancient tree spirits, fairies, and other Nature beings. I feel truly blessed by them. You may resonate with a different type of spirit, or none at all. We are all unique.

Guides as Benefactors in Life

As you learn to deepen your connection to your guides, you discover certain experiences come more easily than others. You may develop an enhanced ability to make money, be in the right place at the right time to help people, or maybe you will feel exceptionally lucky. We are all unique, and our guides are specially chosen to work with us to help us achieve our life goals. Stay as open as possible to your unfolding spiritual path.

Exercise:
Honoring Your Guides

Now you will learn how to open up your heart to see, hear, and feel your guides. If at first you don't succeed, keep practicing. And remember, even if you do not feel them right away, they are aware of you and the efforts you're making to connect with them. You may become aware of contact with them later on.

In your usual meditation spot, make yourself comfortable and bless the space as learned in chapter 1's section Creating Sacred Space. Take several deep breaths and relax.

Focus the breathing on your heart center. As you inhale, visualize white, pink, or green light, similar in nature to the light of your aura, being inhaled or drawn in to your heart. Hold the breath a few moments and then breathe out as you visualize light moving from your heart back out into the world. Smile as you breathe to stimulate joy energy in your heart.

Continue breathing through the heart. Become aware of your body and the way you're sitting or lying down. Feel the physical objects around you and the space in between. Feel the energy fields of your body, your aura, extending away from you. Feel the emerald-green or pink heart light emanating through your aura each time you inhale and exhale.

As you breathe, your energy field is charged with positive energy. As simple as it sounds, once you're paying attention to your psychic development, basic breathing provides energy to help maintain awareness to the presence of your guides. See if you can feel them "tune in" to you as you expand the frequency of your awareness and tune in to them. In a benevolent and kind way, do you feel like you're being watched by your guides? Can you feel them pay attention to you?

In your own personal way, extend a greeting to your guides. They resonate with your energy and life and understand a personal greeting from you best. Say or think or heart-feel whatever is most "you." Repeat your greeting in all directions. Do you feel anything in return, such as a warm wave of calm or joy washing over you, a voice or other sound or song, or a sense of their presence?

If so, allow yourself to be present with them for several moments. Sit with them and learn to recognize the flavor or personality of individual spirits. If not, continue breathing through your heart as before. If heart breathing tires you out, say goodbye to your guides, bless and/or smudge your personal space, and stop the session. When you're ready, continue going about your day but remain alert for any signs of communication.

If you did feel their presence, say to yourself or aloud, "Guides, thank you for sharing my space. If you have any information you wish to share with me, do so now." Maintain an alert state of being as you speak the words. Receive whatever healing or information they wish to share with you. Keep a journal handy to write down any words being shared with you.

When you feel their gifts have been received, ask them whatever questions you wish, tell them about your day, or otherwise share with them. Write things down as they speak or send images into your mind. Once you have made contact, the only thing to break it is your choosing to do so or a lack of attention. So, if while writing things down, you suddenly realize you can no longer hear or sense them, simply start over and breathe through your heart center. You should feel their presence again within a short time.

Once your questions have been answered to your satisfaction, continue being present with your guides until you feel like stopping. Feel the difference in the vibrations and energy fields of your various guides. Do they interact with each other? Does there seem to be a pecking order? Do your guides take turns talking, or do they speak all at once? Do you see how your guides look? How they sound?

When you are ready, thank them for their time and tell them you are breaking contact for the time being. Explain to your guides how grateful you are to have them as helpers in your life. Ask your guides if there is any way you can show them your gratitude. A desire to honor your guides yields *surprising results. A particular guide may ask you to make up with a family member, despite the current perception of who's at fault. Another may ask you to leave a gift under a tree somewhere, pay a bill for someone you meet later on in the day, or otherwise complete a seemingly random act of kindness. Who knows why they ask for such things? My guides never ask me to do anything against my conscience.*

If you feel a guide is asking you to do something against your nature or harmful to others, rest assured the request is not coming from your guides. Be sure you have properly prepared the space for spiritual work as explained earlier in this book. If the problem persists, please refer to the section in the previous chapter about mental illness before moving forward with your practice.

The practice of honoring your guides can be repeated as often as you'd like. A friend shared a powerful practice to help connect to my spirit guides. He suggested that I sit in the same chair at the same time on the same day each week in order to connect to my guides. I felt my guides looked forward to the meeting as much as I did. Over time you don't have to carve out a special time or place to make contact. You learn to naturally maintain contact with them all the time and to be able to ask them something on the fly or listen to an impromptu lecture from them whenever necessary.

Our guides can bestow amazing healing on us and our loved ones. Guides serve as spiritual advisors as we walk our life path. Guides inspire us to new areas of research, love, and joy. Each one is uniquely assigned to each individual human being. It's amazing how harmonious they are to you, specifically. Guides understand your struggles and how to help you succeed in life. Connecting with your guides is a great gift.

Staying Safe

In addition, the more you practice, the more you come into contact with other people's guides. I always set the intention that no one else's guides are allowed to talk to me unless my own guides say it's okay and for my highest good. Setting boundaries keeps random influences away from your life. For healers, learning to talk to other people's guides can greatly assist their work. This skill brings understanding to people's motivations. If you find yourself in a similar situation, remember to ask permission before invading someone else's personal space.

Learning to seal up was one of the best things I ever learned, and it is a very important tool to have in your spiritual tool belt. Now that you're learning to open to the spiritual world around you, do the following exercise to stay protected throughout your day.

Exercise:
Additional Sealing-Up Intention

Anytime you leave a building and go out into the world, take a few moments before you walk out your front door and say to yourself, "I seal up my energy field to stay protected from all harm as I go out into the world. I am protected and safe. If anything in the world wishes to speak to me, you must speak to my guides first. So be it."

You are now protected. If at any time you feel foggy or "loose" energetically, please repeat the exercise to feel more "together" and grounded. As you say the words, really feel your energy field closing off to outside influences. Feel how nice it feels to own your personal space and to be the one who decides what happens inside your energy field.

You have learned to create sacred space, see energy fields, listen to your intuition, honor your dreams, and communicate with your guides. You have all the foundational tools you need to start interacting with the spiritual world-at-large. Remember the chapter on spiritual athletes, too, because the more you delve into the world of spirit, the more energy and strength you need. If you have yet to master any of the exercises you've learned so far, I recommend you continue practicing. There is no race to the finish line. Enjoy the process and take the time to improve your skills.

With consistent practice of all the exercises you've learned so far, you are on your way to integrating your psychic abilities into your everyday life. You're taking significant steps down your personal spiritual path. You're in the midst of a very personal adventure, and your guides can have a major role in shaping your life decisions, all for the betterment of your life. The better you get with the exercises described so far, the easier you'll be able to learn in a self-directed, spiritually guided manner. With experience, you'll gain a thorough understanding of the rules of the spiritual world you've entered.

Part IV

Being Psychic

Chapter Nine

Spiritual Responsibilities

*The whole idea of compassion is based on a keen awareness
of the interdependence of all these living beings,
which are all part of one another,
and all involved in one another.*

—THOMAS MERTON

There is a lot of truth to the cliché "With great power comes
great responsibility." If by now you've learned to see with both
your physical and spiritual senses, you are privy to a lot more
information than you used to receive through your traditional
five senses and body-language interpretation. You are growing
into a bigger version of yourself than you're used to, learning
how to live in your entire being. Your expanded body awareness now includes your aura and extends into less physical
dimensions than you have been used to seeing. Take care of
yourself and treat yourself well. Be loving, kind, and patient,

as you would to a child or spouse. Your spiritual awakening and psychic development will take years—really the rest of your life—before you grow into the rest of who you are. Life is meant to be lived slowly and deeply. Skipping like a stone across the waters of life may get you far, but without the depth of experience, life is empty and incomplete no matter what you accomplish. Better to enrich your life and soul with depth of experience. Variety comes on its own time.

Respecting your abilities—whether mental, physical, emotional, or psychic—is a practical way to honor your unique human self. Honor who you are and what you have learned. Spiritual gifts are truly gifts. Treasure them. Your spiritual gifts guide you in a way you never knew existed. Your abilities are there to help *you* in particular on *your* special path through life. Following your heart leads you to endless depths of compassion and joy. It may sound trite to read these words, thinking it's such a simple path to travel to unlock your spiritual gifts. All I can say is if it were so easy, the world would be a very different place. We humans are masters at complicating things and creating new distractions. It takes great effort to simplify things and take responsibility for our own path.

Take Care of Yourself

The most important thing to take care of on the spiritual path is you, from body to spirit. Many people embark upon a spiritual path to become of service to the world in some way. In any other field it's understood that caring for others is impossible without taking care of yourself first. A football player, no matter how devoted he is to the success of his team, knows the only way he'll be an integral part of the team is if he takes care of his body, gets enough rest, and studies the rules of his craft. Even airplane safety manuals ask us to put the oxygen masks on ourselves first, and then the person next to us. So remember to love yourself enough to ensure you are strong in all areas of your life before helping others.

Our spiritual guides can help us learn to be fully developed human beings and productive members of society. Additionally, our own higher self, the pure spirit part of us always connected to our spirit guides and the source of our intuition, is always available to help guide us through life. Finally, a significant influence on our spiritual path is Mother Earth herself. The food and water we ingest, the air we breathe, the electromagnetic fields we walk through, and everything else Earth provides affects our development. Through the gift of life we experience the illusion of separation and duality, experience emotions both positive and negative, and experience independent free will in a unique way.

In exchange for using her body to house our spirits, when we die we leave our physical bodies here on Earth filled with memories of everything we experienced in life. Our life experiences are full of energy and provide food for the earth's own spiritual development. It's a win-win situation for everyone and everything involved.

As a blossoming spiritual athlete, be grateful for your body and take care of it. Respect and honor the fact you are alive in the way you live your life. Be mindful of your insights. Your higher self and your entire spiritual team of guides are ready to help you in any way they can and feed you as much information as you can handle. Pay attention to what they tell you and take care of yourself. You have a responsibility to honor your body, mind, emotions, and spirituality. Until your own affairs are in order, don't worry about helping other people unless *you* are absolutely inspired to do so. There is no obligation. Once you have your own house in order and you are an effective Good Householder, then you can decide what to do with the rest of the world.

The spiritual world is as full of life as the material world we're so used to. Some life is stationary or local, like a group of plants or animals might be in our world. Some spirits are very mobile like we are. Some even travel with particular people. There are forms of life traveling with people as their protectors, friends, and guides. There are forms of life traveling independently, too, each with its own personality. Some are just passing through, so to speak, while others are part of larger tribes. Each tribe has its own culture and purpose for being here. We share the planet with many life forms we cannot normally see. As with humans, some of these spiritual beings are benevolent.

Others are indifferent to our situation for a variety of reasons, and generally speaking do not get involved in our lives. There are also some beings full of negative energy that inspire hopelessness and despair, feelings of being unsettled or watched, and other creepy feelings. A small group of spirits actively works against the interests of humanity.

Watch out for the last group of spirits, which feed on the weak and confused, on the innocent and open. If spirits *see* you can *see*, and you are watching or noticing them, then in their culture spirits have a right to interact with you. Some of these spirits are involved in our daily life. A negative spirit could manifest as a force gently pushing someone to decide to commit a crime if they've been wavering. These dark energies gravitate to low-vibrational people and situations and thrive in chaotic situations.

Avoid negative people and chaotic situations, and learn to seal up perfectly so nothing can *see* you when you don't want to be *seen*. Always listen to the intuitive guidance of your higher self. Listen to its advice and warnings. If you get the sense you shouldn't go somewhere, or you shouldn't work for a particular company, listen to the guidance even if there is no logical reason to agree. Don't think about it; don't analyze it or weigh the pros and cons. Just listen right away. Learn to trust your intuition. Listening to your intuition is the best way to take care of yourself as you travel your personalized spiritual road. You have a responsibility to follow your intuition.

Following your intuition keeps you in a safe environment while you become strong in spirit. After you've learned the skills in *The Way of the Psychic Heart* and are experienced interacting with the spiritual world around you, you won't need to spend as much time focused on protecting yourself during and between practice sessions. The more you practice, the faster you'll understand how to take responsibility for what you see because you'll be able to discern what your intuition and guides are telling you.

The larger world around us isn't used to people being open and compassionate and psychic, just as we are not used to seeing spirits all the time. So start small. Introduce yourself to the plants and animals around you. Leave gifts for spirits you befriend. Send out loving thoughts of introduction to the spiritual world at large. Set intentions before you dream at night to learn from your guides. Let the spiritual world know you are on the scene, so to speak, and ready to positively interact with it for the highest good of everyone involved.

On a personal level, we have a responsibility to honor those who came before us, our physical ancestors. No matter how tragic their lives or how many mistakes they made, your ancestors created the circumstances of your birth. Be grateful, then, and honor your ancestors.

For those ancestors who are still alive, your parents, grandparents, and perhaps great-grandparents, embrace the idea of always honoring and respecting them. In whatever way you can, be kind to your relatives and share your time and energy with the elders in your family. No matter the ups and downs of their lives, your direct ancestors are the reason you exist. Your ancestors may not have accessed their psychic abilities as you have and not understood the results of their actions. But your spiritual gifts can help you understand the forces that shaped your ancestors' lives and possibly provide you with opportunities to help their long-term spiritual journey be easier.

Remember we are all children here. No matter how accomplished in sports, in life, in the arts, or in spirituality, we are as children to the rest of the spiritual world. Earth is a place for spiritual children to learn about themselves and ultimately freely choose the path of love. So be patient and kind with each other. Always be kinder than you feel. This simple commitment could change the world.

Living in such a heartfelt and kind manner brings grace into your life. To me, grace represents surrender and strength in equal measure, and is a gift to those who live their spiritual responsibilities. Through grace you become known to the spirit world in a safe manner. Over time you may receive unsolicited introductions from various spirits you live near. If your energy is always sealed up and you always set intention to only attract what is for your highest good or helpful to your heart and spiritual path, you will be safe. Use your discretion about these interactions.

Mind Your Own Spiritual Business

Once you've learned to *see* with your psychic senses, you are responsible for what you have *seen*. Your insights can have a powerful effect on other people. Therefore, unless you're specifically asked for advice, better to be prudent and conservative with your abilities and keep your perceptions to yourself. Do not shout from the rooftops and brag about your skills. To walk the spiritual path, use compassion and love when dealing with everyone you encounter. One of the most basic ways you can show compassion is by respecting other people's personal space. Seal up as you walk through life and only utilize your expanded perceptions for your own life and goals. Stay open and alert but keep insights you randomly *see* in other people private unless directly asked. I've mentioned the importance of respecting others' privacy in order to drive home its importance. We all have our own learning curve, and we all mature at different rates. The same is true of everyone on Earth. Just because you *see* something about a person doesn't mean they're ready to hear it. Respect their learning process.

Opening up to *see* another person exposes you to whatever energies are affecting them. You feel what the person feels and empathically embody what they are going through. Peering into other people's consciousness can give you headaches or the flu from an unsuspected blast of negative energy, overwhelm you with the burdens people carry in their hearts, or otherwise bring you down. Unless you have an extremely healthy body, "being psychic" all the time can also weaken your adrenal glands and kidneys. Much energy goes into using psychic abilities, and extended, uninterrupted use can have the same effect on the body as running marathons every day. For most people, having psychic skills constantly *on* is not a sustainable way to live and may lead to serious health problems.

On the other hand, people may be drawn to you as you progress along your spiritual path. Increased spiritual vitality and psychic energy make you appear like a bright light to other souls, who consciously or unconsciously are drawn to you like moths are to the flame. Better to seal yourself up before going out into the world. Pick and choose when and where to open up and *see*. Otherwise keep your visions to yourself.

Ultimately, you are responsible for your life choices, as with all other aspects of an adult's life. The subtle difference with spiritual *seeing* is that by opening up to your psychic abilities, you have agreed to see and understand more about life. With understanding comes responsibility. Just as a doctor wouldn't sit idly by and watch someone have a stroke, you may see things happening around you that require immediate attention. You won't feel comfortable observing and walking away; your gifts inspire you to participate in life in new ways.

When you are called to action by spiritual forces, you'll know what to do. Events will prevent themselves in a special way; your intuition or guides will speak to you directly about the situation; or you'll understand what to do via serendipitous events. I feel the call to action as a nervousness in my stomach as the situation builds around me. I have no idea what's to come, and I have to wait for the situation to manifest. The feeling is similar to when my intuition tells me to avoid a certain area, group of people, or situation. I can't ignore it and have to act.

One day as I walked through a parking lot, I had the feeling and kept alert for anything out of the ordinary around me. Within moments a car rushed past me, swerving all over the parking lot. There were people walking around, including children, and I *knew* intuitively, from the one simple swerve, that the driver was drunk. I watched the car pull into a parking space but nobody left the car. I walked closer until I could look through the car windows. A man had fallen over the front seat, passed out.

I went back to my car and waited. I decided to wait until the man woke up and left the lot. I'd follow him until I could find help. I know, not the brightest plan ever invented, but that's all I had. As I relaxed in my car, my thoughts dimmed and I suddenly had a vision of a police car in the neighborhood. I started my car and followed my intuition down the street. Sure enough, I saw a police car. I sped up and flashed my lights at the car until it stopped. I explained the situation, and the officer followed me back to the parking lot, where serendipitously the man had woken up. I pointed out the car to the officer; as soon as the guy left the parking lot, he began swerving again all over the road. The officer pulled him over and arrested him.

The timing of everything that happened felt like a movie. Each plot point manifested as if on cue, in perfect harmony. I felt very strongly pulled to become involved in the situation, which only happened because I could *see*.

"Wouldn't you have done that anyway once you saw someone driving erratically through a parking lot?" you ask. At that time in my life, probably not. Growing up around gangs and urban decay, I learned to mind my own business and keep my head down. I wasn't the type of person to get involved in other people's issues.

At the same time, just because someone is eating a greasy hamburger with a side order of cheesy fries doesn't mean you should go up to them and tell them how to change their life around and reduce their cholesterol. I hope the difference between the two is obvious. If life pulls you into heightened situations, you'll know when to participate. Otherwise, allow people the freedom to learn on their own timeframe.

Those situations are going to be the exception rather than the rule for most people. Remember not to go searching for ways to help people by scanning them, reading their auras, or other invasive methods. Meddling in other people's affairs just because you can isn't cool, and people will get upset with you.

Last holiday season my family and I were invited to a friend's house for a holiday get-together. Another gentleman had also been invited. He immediately introduced himself as a medium and told my wife how special she was. As the night wore on, he shared stories of times he stopped random people in public to tell them a random psychic insight. Whether he was at a grocery store or restaurant, no one was safe. He was very proud of his skills and did not notice the uncomfortable vibe in the room. As we ate, he proceeded to discuss his insights about other people without asking permission first. He represented the epitome of what not to do on the spiritual path. It's like a psychotherapist telling customers sitting around them in a restaurant what is wrong with them or what they should do with their lives as the customers try to enjoy a pleasant meal. It is very exciting to learn to see with your spiritual eyes, but remember to respect others' personal space.

The more open you become, the more your general sensitivity increases. You may feel more emotional, sentimental, compassionate, joyful—even depressed, angry, afraid, and moody. The experience at first often amplifies how you already feel. The process is different for everyone, but longterm the trend moves toward more joy and love-filled, happy feelings.

In my youth I saw auras around everything alive, from people and animals to plants. The more alive I realized everything was, the harder it was for me to eat food. It sounds crazy, but I felt responsible for the death of everything I ate. I didn't like participating in killing other living beings, not even lettuce. I think it's pretty funny now, but at the time I was very confused. My sensitivity to life was too intense, and I reached an unbalanced point where I could no longer accept death. I cared too much for other life to support my own life. Once I accepted that we live in a temporary world where everything lives and everything dies, I was able to move past my existential crisis and eat guilt-free.

A similar sensitivity can happen when people ask you for advice or a reading. Looking compassionately into their life and history, you may see solutions to their problems. While these solutions may seem easy to implement from your perspective, those solutions may seem insurmountable to them. Don't be fooled by their struggle and reach a point where you start to care more about healing their pain than for allowing their process to unfold. We all learn on our own time in our own ways, each of which is great. Live the adage of teaching others to fish rather than fishing for them. Everyone involved continues to grow.

I used to think that I cared more about the other person's life and loved ones than the person did. Developing deep compassion for other people's process puts you in a more balanced perspective. If someone really cared about a particular problem, they most likely would have already fixed it themselves. Humans are very resilient and intentional creatures and have the power to change their lives for the better, or the worse.

Luckily, we're not required to get caught up in everyone's drama. Just like a doctor can't heal everyone or a conservationist can't save every piece of land or a vegetarian can't save every animal, so too no psychic can respond to every energetic dysfunction in the world.

Aligning With Life

Timely and unusual things start happening to you once you've embarked upon your spiritual journey. When strange coincidences, unexpected situations, and once-in-a-lifetime opportunities become everyday reality, we have a spiritual responsibility to listen to these messages and act accordingly. Sometimes we are called to serve in unusual ways, but ultimately the world will be a better place if we listen and follow the call.

A woman was dying of alcoholism. It had gotten so bad that she was in the hospital and wasn't expected to live much longer. Relatives had been in and out of the hospital all day. Someone with psychic abilities visited the woman to pay her last respects. When the visitor arrived, the woman was not doing well at all and barely spoke. For one of the few times in her adult life, the woman was completely sober, and terrified of her impending death.

The visitor realized this was an important moment and psychically *saw* the woman's impending death. The visitor felt she'd arrived to help the woman through the dying process. The woman's family was gone. The visitor felt called to be present for her final moments.

The two held hands; by the look in her eyes, it was obvious that the woman knew she was about to die. The visitor explained the death process from a psychic perspective, and the dying woman nodded. The visitor told her to stay focused on the brightest light she saw. The woman nodded and wept.

In the next few moments, the woman faded away and died, all the while holding the visitor's hand. Needless to say, the experience was profound for both of them.

From a spiritual perspective, the timing of their meeting was no accident. The visitor felt guided each step of the way. She felt called to participate in the woman's transition to the other side of life; the signs and serendipitous circumstances were so obvious to the visitor. When the situation presented itself, the visitor chose to fully participate in the experience, despite the uncomfortable nature of the situation.

Being spiritually called to help is very different from enabling. Enablers help someone do something the person could have done for themselves, while helpers help someone do something they couldn't have done themselves. The difference is fine but significant. Just because you see a problem doesn't mean it's yours to solve. Getting involved often removes an opportunity for someone else to learn a lesson. Having a well-developed intuition ensures you don't fall down the slippery slope of enabling those around you.

Another aspect is being responsible for where you put yourself in the world. For example, at first you may have difficulty turning the ability off or otherwise filtering what and how you *see*. Learning to open a psychic ability is a different process from learning to close it. As mentioned earlier, in the world of spirit, what you *see* can *see* you too. And when spirits *see* you back, if you're not sealed up, awkward things can happen.

Remember to seal up first to keep as protected as possible. As I grew older and more experienced, I learned to shield myself from negativity and avoid spots of highly negative energy. Since I had learned to *see*, I felt responsible for what I *saw*. I felt required to stay away from places with feeder spirits. Everybody is different, so you'll have to decide for yourself how to handle such things.

Before I learned to seal up completely, I attracted a very motley crew of personalities. Homeless people regularly came up to me for advice, not money. Very mentally and emotionally troubled people came to talk to me. In a large group of people, I was always the one person the religious extremist gave pamphlets to. I asked my guides to help me change the pattern into something better for me. My guides taught me to control my energy field better and focus on sealing up. Learning to shield my energy field from others changed the quality of such experiences moving forward. My particular destiny wove threads of service into many of those experiences, but you may have a different experience.

Along with sealing up and learning to mind your own spiritual business is the practice of *detached presence*. Detached presence means you understand you are not responsible for helping/healing/changing the world while still living in the world and participating in it. It's a way of knowing what situations are "for you" and which ones aren't. The technique is a variation of what you learned in chapter 5, "Honing Intuition."

Exercise:
Checking In

When you are out in the world and a confusing situation arises, you can always take a moment to "check in" for guidance. Ask whatever comes easiest to you: your intuition, your guides, or some other source of information. Ask yourself, "Is this situation for me?" With a strong intuition, you know in a single heartbeat what the answer is.

Sometimes events can trigger a significant emotional response in us, clouding our ability to *see*. Do the following exercise to try and reach a place of clarity.

First of all, if there are other people involved, tell them you need to take a minute to consider the situation. Think about the situation you are faced with. Go over the facts. Visualize the entire situation in your mind. Really look at what's happening. Be present in order to free yourself of others' potential expectations of you in the situation. Honor the mind's desire to analyze and think.

Then let the situation go. Feel yourself completely present in your body and inhale deeply. Hold your breath for a few moments and exhale. Feel yourself relax in your body. Feel the situation you're in, the people and things around you. Whatever you do, keep breathing slowly and deeply and feel yourself in your body in the moment. There are several ways to check in. Here are a few of the most common ones.

Inhale into your heart and smile, however strongly or faintly you feel comfortable with. Feel your aura and spirit, feel your ability to listen to yourself, your ability to choose. Feel the energy of the room. If you are adept at seeing, attempt to feel/see the lines of energy flowing between everything and everyone involved in the situation. Try to detach from the emotions, the pull of these lines of energy connecting everything and everyone around you.

You always have the power of choice.

Continue breathing into your heart and smiling. There is no attachment, no expectation, and no requirements. Choose whatever you wish to choose. Ask your heart about the situation. Smile at your body and your life. Smile at the lines of energy around you. Is the energy you've tuned in to for you or for someone else? Do you want to participate in what you are seeing and make it a part of your reality? Act accordingly.

If you do not see any lines of energy around you, attempt a similar thing by feeling the vibe in the room. Can you feel everyone else's attachments and expectations, what they want from everything and everyone in the room? Do you feel safe? Obligated? Afraid? Hopeful? Happy? Sad? Confused?

Honor whatever you're feeling. Now breathe into your heart, into the energy existing underneath the current situation, into the energy sustaining you day in and day out. Pic-

ture yourself involved more deeply in the current situation. Do you feel stronger or weaker? Do you feel you are "supposed to" continue participating, or walk away? Which decision makes you feel stronger and which one makes you feel weaker? Continue inhaling into your heart and smiling.

If you neither see nor feel the energy of the situation around you, pull all of your energy and attention into your body. Forget about everything going on around you. Inhale into your heart and smile. Close your eyes. Breathe. Smile. Feel present. Feel your body, its organs and bones. Be present. Breathe.

Perform the Yes/No exercise from the Honing Intuition chapter. Ask yourself what you are supposed to do. When you get your answer, the choice is yours whether or not to act. Your life is yours to live. How do you feel about what's happening? Often, when spiritual forces are at work, you feel calm, even during a difficult situation. You have no obligations to anyone other than you, and ultimately even if you do feel called to participate in a situation, you do not have to.

Combine all of your senses, along with your common sense, to come to your answer. Sometimes the intuition becomes clearer when you become aware of your entire being. How do you feel? What do you think? What does the situation trigger?

Once you've honored your thoughts, feelings, and physical responses, once again try to tap in to your intuitive wisdom. Ask yourself a simple yes/no question, call in your *guides for wisdom, or otherwise try to see if the situation is for you.*

Participate if you feel guided to do so and you feel up to the experience. If you feel called but aren't ready to participate, let all the spirits and guides present with the situation, seen or unseen, sensed or not, know you are not ready and are declining their request for assistance. Make sure you are sealed up, and then walk away with a clear conscience.

If you are not called to participate, let the people around you know as much, and leave.

Granted, backing away is often easier to *see* than to do. Our sense of duty or obligation to family members and friends or a sense of guilt prevents us from *seeing* clearly and compels us to help when we really aren't called to do so. Conversely, impatience, irritation, fear, or self-love prevent us from helping when on some level we know we're called to. Our minds like to play little tricks on us. Take a pause before committing to a decision to prevent making knee-jerk reactions.

Not everything you see is meant for you, so learn when to get involved and when to just keep walking. Sealing up minimizes your involvement in random situations, but being open guides your life to moments where your skills can be used to bring about positive circumstances. With time and experience, it gets easier to know what to do. Welcome to being a responsible member of the spiritual community.

Chapter Ten

Intention

All great acts are ruled by intention.
What you mean is what you get.
—BRENNA YOVANOFF

When we are children, our life is directed by all the adults who care for us, teach us, and help us as we grow into adulthood. Once we're all grown up, we decide what we want to do and how we want to do it. Life is a blank page upon which we write the story of our life.

As we move through our teenage years and really start trying to accomplish our first goals in life, sometimes things work out the way we hoped and sometimes they don't. Have you ever wondered why life can be so inconsistent?

From the perspective of our spiritual path, all existence is energy. There are different qualities of energy; different flavors mix together in myriad ways to manifest the world we see within and around us. There's the energy of the universe co-alescing into galaxies, solar systems, and planets. The energy of life allows us to be here in a body. The way our own energy mixes with the energy of the universe creates our reality.

When we are young, we frequently experience life through the perspective of those raising us. A favorite teacher likes certain music, and so we like it, too. Our parents love eating healthy food, and so we decide to never eat healthy again. The influence of people around us is also a form of energy. We incorporate energy into our life to create our reality. So what does energy have to do with intention?

Intention is a form of energy and combines the mental and emotional programming we've received while growing up. We carry our programming with us like nametags on our chest, affecting how we think and feel about the world. From my perspective, everything we say and do affects our reality, creates our reality. At our current level of consciousness, these thoughts and feelings are the intentions we are using to manifest our reality, from our internal health and energy levels to our external successes and failures in life. We live within a sea of energy and what we currently use to interpret the sea are thoughts and emotions. Our psychic abilities are the boat, sails, and oars to help us travel more wisely through the sea.

There are no accidents. There is only intention. Intention, conscious and unconscious, creates our reality. In the world of business we say, "What gets attention, gets done." In the Bible we read, "As a man thinketh, so he is." These are examples of what I'm getting at. In this chapter we explore how to become conscious creators of our life and learn exercises for helping us get there.

The simple view that we create our reality resonates across different socio-economic strata, across religions and cultures the world over. A key aspect of living a responsible spiritual life is accepting that we are responsible for the quality and character of our life.

Each exercise has helped us open to our spiritual life. We've learned how to improve our ability to focus and concentrate. We needed to improve these two skills in order to really understand and manifest the principles of intention. Whether psychic or not, humans have a great ability to get things done and achieve personal goals. We can already manifest our intentions. Those who have the greatest ability to manifest their intentions are the ones who have the greatest ability to concentrate on their personal goals. Combine the ability to concentrate with an open and active psychic life, and we have the added advantage of engaging our spirit guides and higher self in our quest to achieve our hopes and dreams.

All the skills we've learned so far develop our ability to intend certain things to happen in our life. From saying affirmations, a variation of setting intentions, to completely relaxing the body and becoming more aware of our surroundings, we've been learning how to maintain a high level of concentration on a particular topic for an extended period of time. We've also learned how to tune in to the greater reality in which we live and become comfortable with how our energies interact with the world around us. As we increase our awareness of reality, we are more able to change reality to suit our needs.

I've always believed people always get what they ask for, even if they don't know what they're asking for. I believe everything we as individuals and humanity in general have experienced was intended to happen. There are no victims, no accidents, and no chance events. I see all events as movements of energy designed to best help us as eternal souls grow and wake up to our potential.

As our consciousness, mood, and attention changes throughout our life, moment by moment, our external life mirrors and creates our reality. And what we send out comes back to us for seeming good or ill. The typical state of human consciousness doesn't allow us to actively alter what we've been asking for in our thoughts, feelings, and actions. As we travel the path of our spiritual awakening, however, the skills we've learned allow us to change our reality. Opening to our psychic abilities also allows us to become conscious creators of our reality. As with all skills in *The Way of the Psychic Heart*, their effectiveness is only as good as our abilities to work with them. You are now closer than ever to sitting in your own driver's seat and setting the course your life will take.

You may need time to understand exactly what you are currently asking for. The human psyche is fractured into many different sub-personalities, each with its own hopes and dreams. You are not just one person. You are fractured into many little personalities all vying for dominant intentional expression. Part of you wants to be happy; part of you wants to be right; part of you wants to be the best; part of you wants to be helpful; and part of you doesn't want anything. These various aspects aren't all working together toward a common goal. In order to become more effective at achieving the life you've always dreamed of, you need to better understand who "you" are. The following exercise increases awareness of what is motivating your life circumstances.

Exercise:
Self-Observation

Becoming a conscious being is a long and arduous process. Much work is involved, and many things need sorting out along the way. The deeper you travel down your personal spiritual path, the more you discover aspects of your consciousness working at odds with themselves. Observe these traits. Simply becoming aware of certain physical, emotional, and psychological patterns goes a long way toward eliminating them. Many patterns exist from habit more than from deliberate effort. Some have been programmed into you by family and friends, jobs, and other external experiences on your way from youth to adulthood. This first exercise increases awareness of your personal mental, emotional, and physical habits, and the first step in learning how to set clear intentions.

When you wake up in the morning, after you've written down any dreams, get up and go about your day. No matter what you do throughout the day, watch yourself do it. Go about your day as if you are two people—the one doing the action and the one watching the action happen. At the end of the day, write down any significant observations into a special journal kept just for this exercise. Be as general or detailed as you like. The aim is to record personality traits you've observed having a positive or negative affect on your everyday life. Focus on writing down moments at odds with other moments. For example, if you start the day telling yourself how fun the day will be, and then choose to get mad while driving to work because of the way other people are driving, these are at odds with each other. We choose to have fun; we choose to be mad.

Write down things that make you happy, angry, sad, hopeful, fearful, or any other emotion. Write down when you say something positive. Write down when you say something negative. Write down the things you keep your word about and the things you don't. Write down what makes you tired and what gives you energy. Write down when something you wanted to have happen actually did, and when it didn't. In a nutshell, notice your personality patterns.

Through the exercise, you increase awareness of who you really are and what motivates you. You learn what thoughts and actions, what feelings and opinions you are sending out into the world and which ones you thought you were but actually weren't at all.

Keep a journal for three weeks. The more you use it, the more accurate your view of yourself becomes. When the time is up, go back through the journal and see if you can notice any patterns in your behaviors. Lump them together into different "personalities" and name them. For example, I could lump things into Happy Chad, Arrogant Chad, Peaceful Chad, Scheming Chad, and many others.

Determine how each mini-personality fits into your overall hopes and dreams, plans and schemes. Are all these parts of you working together toward your current goals? If you really want to go back to school, is your entire being helping you go back, or are there parts of you with different ideas about your future?

With practice, self-observation gives a much clearer picture of the current state of your consciousness. Obviously, the more cohesive your consciousness, the more able you are to manifest your intentions. In the same way a company with well-established goals and a well-trained staff is more likely to achieve its goals, so too a person with a centered and directed self can achieve goals that a scattered and unfocused person never could.

Benefits of Intention

The greatest power of the magicians and seers of old was their power of intention. Ancient medicine men and women concentrated so thoroughly, they could manifest the most amazing things, from seeing auras to shape-shifting and beyond. Ancient mystics understood reality is perception and discovered unique ways to interact with the world around them. Even learning to develop psychic abilities is an act of intention. Remember the saying "In order to see magic, you have to believe in it"? If your brain was allowed to believe magic was impossible and that being psychic wasn't an option, you'd be unable to see auras or develop your intuition. You created a reality in which such things did not exist.

I have seen people do some incredible things with their psychic abilities, to the point where the rules of the everyday world dissolve into the realm of myth and magic. And all of their abilities stemmed from the same principles covered in these chapters. You are ready to combine everything you've learned to create your own reality.

I encourage you to repeat the three-week process covered in the last exercise as often as needed for you to truly become aware of all the pieces motivating and guiding your everyday life. As you increase your self-awareness, you are more able to change the direction of your life. Eventually you can see, feel, and sense these mini-personalities arise before their actions or words counter your overall goals in life. By observing yourself on a regular basis, you not only understand more about the patterns and habits defining who you are but also learn to take a pause before acting so you can choose exactly what you want to say or do.

In small yet significant ways, you're ridding yourself of extraneous habits on the path to becoming an even more focused and cohesive person. Stay focused to improve your other psychic abilities and increase the length of time you can practice before tiring. Own your personal space and personal power as a humble yet confident person.

Heart vs. Mind Revisited

Working to develop focus and unity in your consciousness works best when you are living a heart-centered life and following a heart-centered spiritual path. Life provides many opportunities to live a more self-serving than holistic and heart-centered life. The path of the mind is focused more on maintaining the structure of its reality box than on connecting with the larger universe around us. The mind/ego structure is not interested in losing control. The ego encourages us to live only for our own single self. People caught up in ego use others to achieve goals in life but otherwise don't value them.

I have known powerful psychics who chose the path of the mind. Some were great healers; others were incredibly wealthy.

But without the heart, all had overdeveloped egos and focused more on themselves and saw the people and world around them as objects to be used. These people make great, even comical, clichés in a story, but unfortunately in real life such an approach to life left them crippled and blind. One exceptionally gifted healer never kept clients or students because, one after another, everyone began to understand the healer's true personality.

In smaller ways, we all need to stay aware of the differences between doing things for the self at the expense of others and choosing to live as one wheel in the great love machine of life. Learning to see auras or developing a strong intuition is a gateway to much bigger things as our skills develop. But even more so is learning to really become strong with the Heart Breath exercise in chapter 1, living the principles of the spiritual athlete in chapter 2, and aligning yourself with and befriending your spirit guides. These tools keep you on a heart-centered path in life. From the heart you can decide how best to use your intentions to manifest your goals in harmony with the larger world around you.

The next exercise shows how to set intentions for your life. I recommend performing chapter 1's Heart Breath exercise again before you begin.

Exercise:
Setting Intentions

Having a strong center, feeling grounded and heartfelt, is a great help on the spiritual path, and indeed with anything you do in life. Being centered makes all of your efforts and practices so much easier. Feeling grounded and centered from the heart helps your psychic development progress in leaps and bounds. Seeing yourself clearly and becoming focused is energizing. It takes a lot of energy to be scattered.

Let's learn to set major intentions for our lives. We'll set positive intentions in alignment with the greatest benefit for all involved, helping all and harming none. Setting negative intentions is a common mistake people make because we often focus on what we don't want instead of what we do want. We say things like "I'll never drink again" instead of "From now on, I choose to care for my body's health and well-being." People in general pay more attention to what's bothering them than to what feels good. Learning how to properly set intentions is one way we can learn to see life in a more positive light.

The best intentions are the shortest ones. Focus on the overall intention rather than the specific details. Use as few words as possible to describe your goals.

You need a small notepad and a comfortable place to practice.

As usual, find a place to sit in private, take several deep breaths, and relax. Become aware of your body and the environment you are in. Be present and smile.

Observe your life thus far. Where are you? Are you as happy, successful, comfortable, joyful, and fulfilled as you want to be? If so, reflect upon how you arrived here. What circumstances helped manifest your current life? What did you do or not do to get here? Condense your life experiences into a few sentences or self-affirmations. Write your affirmations down on the front page of your small notepad. These intentions led you to your current life. Honor and recognize these perspectives because, for better or worse, they've helped create a person ready to become a more conscious spiritual being.

If you aren't where you want to be, then where do you want to be? Where do you want to be next month, next year? In five years? What do you want out of life? Do you want to know what you are here for? Do you want a lover to share life with? Do you want financial freedom? Whatever your intention, form a **one-sentence** *statement about each goal and write it down on the first page of your notepad. Don't go on and on for days about the details; you'll dilute the original intent with the mind's desire to control the outcome.*

Once you are finished, review your list. These are your long-term intentions.

Write down your future goals next. Be as specific yet as succinct as possible. Condense each goal into one sentence. Every morning when you arise, after you write down your dreams, speak these intentions aloud. Always end by letting your spirit guides know you are open to receiving guidance about your new intentions.

On the second page, write down the personality traits you wish to cultivate in order to achieve these goals. Again these could be anything, from "I am holy" to "I always embrace daily responsibilities" to "I study Spanish Monday, Wednesday, and Friday" to "I am positive, trustworthy, and true."

Based on your self-observations from the previous exercise, which of these traits are the ones keeping you from fulfilling your dreams and goals? Is the problem a lack of effort, the fear of failure, a sense of unworthiness, or the inability to follow through? Take the top reasons and write them down as positive affirmations. For example, instead of writing down, "I promise to stop procrastinating," say, "I am happy to make the time and effort to achieve my personal dreams." Instead of saying, "I'll stop being so negative," say, "I am happy all the time." Write what you want instead of what you don't want in order to ensure the changes you want to make in your life come across in a positive light. Stay focused on what you want instead of what you don't want.

Keep your list with you wherever you go. I had a little 3" x 5" memo book in my back pocket full of my intentions. Whenever you lose focus, pull out your notepad and read or speak your intentions. Repeat as often as you need to. Send your intentions from your heart out into the world.

People always get what they ask for, whether they know what they're asking for or not. Learning to set intentions is a great way to train yourself to stay focused on what you want. The more present and centered you are, the easier you will be able to manifest intentions.

Will vs. Intention

Will and intention can be easily confused, so let's define the terms. *Will* is the part of you forcing something to happen. We use willpower to push the body to do three more reps at the gym or skip dessert if we're trying to lose weight. We push through our limits and make something happen. Will is a very extroverted act and doesn't stop until the goal is achieved. There is no yielding, and we only parry or feint from our goal strategically, hoping such a move gets us closer to our goal from a new angle. Willfulness is a very attack-oriented approach.

Intention is more passive. Intention actively asks for something to happen yet simultaneously yields to the process of reaching the intended goal as well as to the form intention takes. Intention works best when things are asked for energetically. For example, instead of asking for a job at such-and-such corporation making x salary, ask the universe to provide you with a job and income big enough to become a stronger person and help you along your spiritual path. You're still being very specific but unattached to the external form. Intention gets to the heart of the matter and cares more about how the job affects you as a person than how it looks on the surface. Intention requires that we exist in a very receptive state of consciousness.

Being specific with the goal of making the world a better place is an important distinction, because walking your spiritual path, practicing your skills, and living from the heart magnifies your intention. Use the additional stored energy to help you through situations. You can force things to happen your way to your detriment. Better to set intentions and let the universe send things to you in a gentler, more constructive, and often much more surprising manner. We are all children learning how to grow up compared to what we'll remember once our physical body dies. Remember: the host of spiritual beings here to help you has access to information. Intending things and then letting our helpers bring us to the most beneficial solution is more harmonious in the long run.

Our psychic intuition can provide us with a lot of insight, but sometimes we don't know the correct questions to ask in order to receive the best information we need to reach our goals. Turning our intentions over to a higher power, from God/Goddess to our spirit guides, allows things to come to us for our highest good in a way unaffected by our limitations.

There are many cautionary tales about powerful people, real or imaginary, who willed things to happen to their detriment. Overreaching willfulness is the basis of many "bad guys" in fantasy tales. Darth Vader wanted to use his will (the Dark Side) to prevent death. Lord Voldemort basically tried to do the same thing. Even one of Pythagoras's students suffered from an overactive will, and his name was Milo.

Milo of Croton had a natural talent for strength, so Pythagoras showed him certain techniques to enhance his natural strength. He carried a calf around on his back as strength training. Eventually the calf became a bull, and Milo was still able to carry it. Some thought he was a reincarnation of Hercules; his strength was so mighty. He won five Olympiads in a row, but arrogance finally led to his demise. One day Milo came upon a tree and a woodsman. The woodsman trapped two wedges while trying to cut down the tree. Milo decided to use his willpower to split the tree apart by hand and remove the wedges for the woodsman. Milo removed the wedges, but then the tree snapped shut and cut off his forearms, and he died. Another version of the story states that when Milo attempted the same task, his arms became stuck in the tree, and eventually a pack of wolves descended upon him and ate him up.

Milo's is an extreme case of the overuse of will. Just because we have the power to do something doesn't mean we should attempt to do it. Use your willpower wisely, as it has the power to change the world around you in significant ways. A strong ego always rationalizes the use of will to bring about a desired goal. Conscious intention submits to a higher will and understands all aspects of a situation. Remaining humble and checking in with intuition before taking action toward your intentions ensures you remain heart-centered in your walk through life. Remain open to adjustments in the manifestation of your intentions: the heart can flow with life, but the ego likes to control things. Being one who yields to a higher power is an important part of manifesting your intention.

Intention vs. Being Literal

A barrier to receiving what we've asked for in our intentions is expectation. As mentioned, setting an intention, which is a form of energy, has an effect like a boomerang and works best with no expectation of its form upon returning into your life.

Being extremely specific with your intentions can lead to frustrations, and often puts the focus too much on a literal form than on the spirit of what you're asking for. Use caution when setting intentions. With your increased ability to focus and concentrate, you are developing the power to get whatever you want. Being overly literal about what you want puts constraints on the spiritual world and limits its ability to give you what you want. Get to the core of what you want.

Intention vs. Action

We live in a much larger world than we realize. Spiritually, many people, situations, and spiritual influences help us achieve our dreams. I am constantly surprised at the twists and turns in life that provided exactly what I needed to become the person I am today.

So, how does setting intention actually lead to getting a job? What is the purpose of setting an intention?

Putting your deepest desires in sentence form and reading them aloud for the spiritual world to hear is the first step in manifesting something. Once the intention is set and you read your words aloud each day, your repetitions set events in motion. So pay attention to what happens next. You may have a lot of work to do.

For example, when I set an intention for something, my intuition is right there with me. As I state my intention aloud, my intuition is right there chattering away with an entire laundry list of things I need to do in order to make intention a reality. With the help of my intuitive guidance, I'm asked to play an active part in the manifestation of my goals and dreams.

Setting intentions is a receptive but active task, and once the universe knows what we want to achieve, it conspires to help create our new reality. We are co-creators in life, and we cannot sit back and do nothing and expect everything to happen on its own. We don't suddenly wake up one morning with a new job, realize how to get there and what our position is, and fit right in with no prior efforts. No, we update the résumé, go to the interview, accept the job, and then show up for work. When opportunity arises, we take action to bring opportunity to life. I believe intention brings opportunities our way, but as co-creators, we have free-will choice whether or not to act on a particular opportunity.

Taking action is where some people fall short. Some people use intentions as a way of passing the buck on life. People can feel safe in the belief they've done their job because they've set intentions; all other action is up to the universe. If the intentions don't become reality, then such people believe it wasn't meant to be. Hands are washed of the process of manifestation. Setting intentions is a simple concept, but sitting on the sidelines of your life and waiting for change to come to you can be a self-defeating behavior.

Living a spiritual life isn't meant to supersede our everyday life; the spiritual life includes our everyday life in every way. I really like the following Zen saying: "Before enlightenment, chop wood, carry water. After enlightenment, chop wood, carry water." In part, this means gaining ground on a spiritual path does not exempt us from carrying out our daily responsibilities. Remember the principles of the Good Householder. Be a part of the world and take care of your earthly duties. If you aren't happy with your current life duties, set new intentions and then listen for guidance about how to achieve these goals.

Intuition is a powerful ally as you seek out new opportunities in life, whether in love, career, or other creative endeavors. So are your spirit guides. My spirit guides help bring in opportunities for me to engage, whereas intuition tells me what to do to maximize opportunities already present in my life. An active spiritual life provides you with everything you need to manifest your intentions. Through self-observation you discover impediments to effective action, habits preventing you from achieving your goals. Setting intentions helps you reach goals. And you are the one responsible for making your reality. Actively participating in the process takes into account the necessity to surrender our intentions out into the world and the importance of not forcing things to happen beyond the desires of the heart. But surrendering and yielding do not negate our duty to take action; we simply need to wait for opportunities while remaining heart-centered. Remaining heart-centered aligns us with the universal principles of helping all and harming none, and keeps us in the proper state of being prior to taking action.

The magic of heartfelt intention is in the combination of surrender and action. In the final chapter, we'll explore how joyful living and deep surrender are the keys to a happy life supporting your ever-growing psychic abilities.

chapter eleven

The Joyful Life

Joy is not in things; it is in us.
—RICHARD WAGNER

Many spiritual paths teach living a joyful life. Joy really is the key to everything life has to offer. From overcoming obstacles to finding your life's loves, joy is the guiding light leading you along your spiritual development. The most exuberant and loving spirits I've met have all preached the same thing: the meaning of life is joy. Living a joyful life is the whole point. Engage in loving relationships, do actively joyful things at work and in the world, love yourself, and find happiness.

Obviously, being psychic is not a prerequisite to finding joy. People find joy without ever seeing auras or having any psychic experiences whatsoever. Still, if you're now one who can *see*, you will be exposed to a lot of things formerly hidden from you. Joy is your ally on your blossoming, ever-unfolding spiritual path.

The Protective Power of Joy

Joy offers protection from many of the negative influences in life. Live in alignment to attract joyful life experiences and steer clear of the dark areas of life. Joy keeps you protected from seemingly random acts of negativity. Joy shields your energy field from heavy energy, and such things won't be attracted to your field. It's said misery loves company. So does joy. But joy and misery are like oil and water and never mix. Therefore, focus on joy to protect you from the negativity in life.

Joy is also close cousins with humor. Many apparent tragedies are transformed by joy into comedies. The quality of your life is in large part based on your perspective, and the joy perspective feels the best to me. Finding joy in life is more fun. Laughing at myself when I do silly things helps me learn not to take life so seriously. No matter what happens "to" you, joy transforms these experiences into something better. Things fall into place and sync up with joy.

I've also noticed the spirit world has a wonderful sense of humor. The higher the vibration, the greater the sense of humor and joyfulness you will experience. We sense this effect in life. We say someone who's moping around, pointing out all the misery in the world, has a "heavy vibe" or is "down in the dumps." Their energy is dense and thick. Conversely, those who skip along through life with a twinkle in their eye and are quick to smile are fun to be around. We say happy people are "high on life" or "uplifting to be around." The psychic world is the same way. There are really dense and heavy spirit beings in the world and very light, joyful, and refined beings, too. Our unique personality attracts kindred spirits, just as our thoughts attract our reality.

Joy curbs an overdeveloped ego. The ego is our mental sense of self. The mind's job is to create a safe reality box within which we live. As we grow spiritually, we reach a place where we can safely move beyond the protection of the mind and walk into the protection of something much larger—our heart. Joy flows freely in heart-centered people because the natural expression of a happy heart is joy. Joyful living keeps the ego in check by minimizing its importance to our development. The ego has served its purpose and provided us with a safe environment within which we took our first steps on our spiritual path. We always honor who we are, but now we're ready for something connecting us to the world in truly magical ways.

Joy is one of those magical, heart-centered spiritual-emotional states of being that deeply affects the mind and ego. One who is filled with joy is less attached to the particulars of life. Joyful people are easily able to flow from one experience to the next, in a natural sync with their intuition. Being joyful keeps us in the moment, present to whatever is happening. Therefore we naturally, gradually, and safely become less attached to grasping or longing for specific things in life. Led by joy, we understand how surrender works in helping us achieve our goals. We see how everything connects together and makes sense.

Joyful people choose to be joyful, and are wonderful to be around. With commitment, everyone can learn to be more joyful. At times our psychic experiences can be overwhelming. Many people seek spirituality from a sense of hopelessness, longing, or loss. As our psychic abilities develop and we learn to see new and amazing things like auras and spirits, our energy resonates with our emotional and psychological state of being. If we aren't living a joy-filled life, then what we see may not always be so pleasant. However, the more joyful we choose to be, the more positivity we attract back into our lives. Eventually, joyful living becomes our state of being. Living joyfully can feel like we've reached nirvana.

Learn to protect and own your personal space to keep out negative influences interfering in your life. If you learn the two skills of cultivating joy and protecting your personal space, then you'll shield out the bad and only allow in the light, no matter how small.

Even so, unpleasant psychic experiences may happen. There was a time when my psychic abilities showed me spirits and energies in the world that left me feeling depressed. I tuned in to the pain and suffering of the world more than the joy. I focused on people's problems instead of their accomplishments. I focused on the many environmental tragedies happening to the planet and saw the world as a victim of human ignorance. I couldn't see we, too, serve the earth, no matter how strange we seem to be acting at the moment.

Sometimes we have to agree to see things joyfully, to choose to focus on the positive over the negative. Feeling joy can take real effort. There are many entrenched habits we need to let go of before joy becomes the dominant force of our existence. I'd even go so far as to say joy is more important than love in a spiritual life, because through joy we find so many positive life circumstances—including love, to be sure, but also career paths and other meaningful aspects of our lives.

The first exercise below moves us to a more joyful path in life. The exercise is something we can literally do every minute of every hour we are awake each day.

Exercise:
Smiling

Sometimes the simplest things have the most profound effects on our life. This exercise is the simplest one in the whole book, and it goes like this:

Smile.

The end.

Silly, huh? Smile wherever you go, no matter what you do. The most basic experience of joy is smiling. So smile. Gently raise the corners of your mouth and feel how your entire perspective on life changes.

In college I found a book by Mantak Chia called *Awaken Healing Energy through the Tao.* The book is full of amazing information on how to increase energy flow through the body, but I learned about the benefit of smiling from Chia. In many exercises, students begin by holding a gentle smile. Smiling feels good, and soon I was smiling as I drove, walked to school, hiked; basically anytime I could remember to, I smiled.

I noticed when I wasn't smiling, it was harder to be happy. Shocking, right? To be sure, the connection between smiling and happiness is obvious. If so, why do so few people smile? The connection between smiling and joy is important. A happy mind is more open to change, and change is a constant in the world of spirit. Developing your psychic abilities puts you in alignment with your spiritual path by focusing your attention on a larger *you* than you're used to seeing.

Sometimes we see unpleasant things. It is difficult to continue your spiritual path and expand your psychic abilities without coming face to face with some of the things holding you back in life. As we learned with the self-observation exercise from the last chapter, becoming aware of something changes it, and the spiritual path is a path of consistently increasing personal awareness. Expanding awareness causes changes to happen in our lives, and ultimately leads to an opening of our heart center. An open heart center cultivates joyful living. Eventually, no matter where you start on the path of spiritual and psychic development, you will come to a place of joy.

Don't worry if you are not joyful all the time. Ultimately we'll be on the spiritual path for the rest of our lives. If we continue practicing, we continue becoming more heart-centered and joyful. Months or years pass; time doesn't matter. The point is to allow yourself to be joyful as much as you are able to, as often as you can remember. Surrender to joy's positive influence, and your life transforms in positive and surprising ways. Your intentions manifest more easily, for example. Being happy and joyful is also relaxing. Being relaxed is a key to calming the mind's thoughts and allowing the heart to lead us. Spirit responds to our intentions. Smile and be joyful. Joy is both a way of life and a powerful intention. When you put joy out into the world, you draw joy back in.

As we learn to increase joy in our lives, we discover it's easier to *see* and interact with our spirit guides. We become less dense beings, and our psychic sight clarifies. As our energy level and quality of character changes in life, the makeup of our group of spirit guides changes. Let's learn more about how our guides can help us lead a more joyful life.

Soul Families

We have our birth family, and then we have our soul family. Our birth family is connected by blood, but our soul family is connected by energetic lines of spirit running just as deep. Your soul group is the main group of people you interact with in your life.

The people you resonate with may not be your direct blood relatives. Many people find comfort in a special group or groups of friends and family. Friends travel from state to state building their careers and lives separately but near one another. Soul groups also include aunts or cousins who feel more like parents and brothers and sisters than your own immediate family. Welcome to your soul family.

Depending on many circumstances, your soul family can also have a negative influence in your life. I believe we live over and over again, life after life, in different bodies in different parts of the world as we move through the long process of our spiritual awakening. Along the way we've forged these deep and long-lasting relationships with a large group of other souls, our soul family. When those relationships delve into the darker side of the human experience, some of these experiences carry through into our present incarnation.

If you find yourself in such a situation, surrounded by the negative influences of people you also deeply care about, then I recommend practicing the exercises from chapter 1 more frequently, especially the Heart Breath exercise, and really try to cultivate joy in your current life, even by the simple act of smiling more. Through your own efforts, you will become free of these negative connections. Perhaps you've embarked on your spiritual path in order to free yourself of negativity and move into a more joyful way of living. The choice is yours to make, even if actualizing your intentions takes many months or years of effort.

Love can be brought into a negative situation even if the events surrounding happened long ago in another lifetime. The following exercise connects you with the soul family in your life and helps you make peace with them.

Exercise:
Soul Connections

Requirements: Quiet setting, pen and paper, comfortable clothing.

As usual, find a quiet, comfortable place to sit and take several deep breaths to relax and become centered. Feel yourself completely within your body: your skin, bones, blood, organs, hair, clothes, and all the rest. Feel the room around you—its shape and texture, the air and sounds, the shapes of all the objects near you.

Invite your spirit guides to join you. Feel their presences, their various personalities and essences. Allow yourself to remember more about them each time you meet. Offer a greeting and thank those who chose to join you for being present during your practice.

Let your guides know you want to see the energy lines connecting you to your living soul family (many members of your soul family are not in bodies but instead are helping you and your soul family as spirit guides). Visualize everyone you know, everyone you work with or see on a regular basis, along with extended family members you know. Ask your guides to show you in some way those who are part of your soul family.

Seeing these connections can be emotional. You may spontaneously remember past lives with members of your soul family. You may feel ill about certain people or anger for no logical reason. No matter what arises, inhale deeply and let the negativity pass. There will be time to return to these memories later. Inhale deeply and pull all those emotions together into your solar plexus. Feel all the past and future joys and sorrows.

With the help of your guides, exhale all energy back into the universe. You can send it wherever's easiest: into the ground, the sky, the sun, a surrounding forest, lake or meadow, to God/Goddess, or wherever you want. As you exhale, smile and allow your body to relax more deeply. Continue practicing until there are no more tensions remaining toward anyone in your life.

When as much of the tension has passed as you can exhale, stand up. Your eyes can be open or closed, whichever helps you concentrate best while keeping your balance. Place your hands together in front of your heart and smile. Begin facing North and say aloud, "I am sorry to everyone in my soul family for any unhappiness, stress, or pain I have caused you in the past, present, or future. Please forgive me as I forgive myself for these misunderstandings. I was still a child and did not understand what I was doing. I will share my love and peace with all of you to the best of my ability. Amen."

Continue to the East, South, and West. Say the words to the sky above and to all those souls about to come into their bodies.

Then look down upon Mother Earth and say, "Dear Mother Earth, I am grateful for this opportunity to be with you in body again. Thank you so much for taking care of all your children so well. I apologize for ever disrespecting you in the past; I was still a child and did not understand what I was doing. As I continue my spiritual journey with you, I wish to be a vessel of peace and joy in the world. Please help me understand what I can do to make the world a better place for everyone and everything alive."

Now, close your eyes if you haven't already. Say a silent prayer of gratitude for yourself, for everything you've accomplished so far, for every lesson you've learned. Pick a few things to work on and say a silent prayer to your guides for help with these things. When you are done, inhale, smile, and open your eyes as you exhale.

Remember to thank your guides for helping you, and end the exercise. As the drama of life unfolds, find opportunities to bring joy to a painful relationship with another person

*and heal old wounds. The more you can find opportunities
to bring joy and healing into the world, the better. You become free to be more joyful and abundant.*

*When you are done with the exercise, write down every-
thing you remember about your soul family. Many tensions
and attachments you feel to certain people have a foundation
in the distant past. The soul-connection exercise sheds those
bonds and leaves you feeling free to create new positive experiences with other people.*

Do the exercises as often as necessary. Life constantly
changes, and triggering issues may continue to manifest. You
can approach the world with more love and respect by releasing
the negativity found within your soul family. Distancing yourself from negative people and influences is a simple way to bring
more joy into your life.

Sometimes doing healing exercises feels like opening a gigantic can of worms full of negative energy. There could be a
lot of pent-up energy in your relationships with certain people.
Soon after you perform the exercise, someone in your soul family may trigger or challenge you. Tests that appear as you try to
clear negative energy from your life are pretty common. Just do
the best you can to handle the situation as joyfully as possible
and move on. These situations may surround you for the rest of
your life, but choose to see them joyfully—and suddenly you've
turned lemons into lemonade. When you fully engage in joyful

living, you see the positive in every situation. Viewing life situations from a joyful perspective removes your attachment to any situation, and you are able to see things clearly. Your psychic abilities help you *see* why members of your soul family suffer from attachment to negative situations. Be loving and kind to them when you do have to interact with them and avoid them the rest of the time.

Forgiveness and Joy

Learning forgiveness opens your heart to experience more joy. Applied externally to the relationships in your life, forgiveness brings a lot of healing. Your sense of duty and attachment to others diminishes and patterns disappear. You free yourself of the burden caused by negative human relationships.

On the flip side, learning self-forgiveness is an even more powerful way to extricate ourselves from negative life situations. We are really our own worst critic. What a burden we place on ourselves when we refuse to move on from the mistakes we've made in life. Our desire for perfection and the mind's wish to have everything conform to its rules can confound our attempts to experience real joy in life. Self-criticisms, self-doubt, self-pity, and wishing history had been different leave no room for joy in life.

We are all little children in the world of spirit. We are just starting out on our journey; otherwise we wouldn't be here. Give yourself a break. Make a mistake; that's how we best learn. Our reality is full of apparent separation, contrast, and duality. Contrasts, whether between right and wrong or good and bad, for example, are designed to help us connect with our center and move forward along our spiritual paths. When we hold on to less than satisfactory life experiences, we constrict the natural flow of life energy within. When life energy is constricted, we stagnate and become heavier and heavier, which drags us into a deep cycle of negative self-image.

I love the concept of *wabi-sabi*, a Japanese term meaning "an intuitive way of living emphasizing finding beauty in imperfection, and accepting the natural cycle of growth and decay." Wabi-sabi embodies a balanced and practical worldview. Wabi-sabi embraces our imperfection as a matter of course. Embracing such a concept releases attachment to particular life events and allows our life energy to flow once again. Joy is allowed back into our hearts when the energy of life is flowing.

Surrender Meditation

Another helpful practice to let life's stresses fall by the wayside is the surrender meditation. Surrender meditation is a way of opening to change that also provides insight into everything you thought you knew about who you are and what motivates you. The surrender meditation is a peculiar technique difficult to describe. Done correctly, surrender meditation is a powerful way to merge with your higher self and really let a lot of your earthly burdens fall away. Your burdens are naturally replaced with ecstatic joy. Surrender meditation is a way of deeply remembering who you really are and brings your waking consciousness to the realm your spirit guides call home.

I spontaneously entered into a surrender meditation while meditating before bed one night. Something released in me and I experienced a state of ecstasy. Utter joy filled my heart, and tears of gratitude rolled down my cheeks. All of my spirit guides helped amplify the experience, and I felt surrounded by unconditional love. Spiritual energy filled my room, and I felt like I was on cloud nine. I continued focusing on my breathing and the feeling of pulsing energy in my spine, and the feeling kept increasing. My body spasmed and arched to the rhythmic energy flowing up my spine. The presence of my guides in the room was palpable. I had no idea what was happening to me. I did some research and happened upon the works of St. John of the Cross, St. Thérèse of Lisieux, and other saints. These saints described similar symptoms as religious ecstasy. I understood their description of ecstasy, but I wasn't particularly religious.

Every time I meditated, the ecstasy returned. Eventually, underneath the blissful feeling, I felt like something was trying to break out of my body. I made animal noises, constantly cleared my throat, and arched my back like a cat. I felt like I was bigger than my body yet trapped in my body at the same time.

My dreams and psychic abilities increased dramatically, and my dream life was rich with encounters with spirits of all types. As my meditations became more intense, so did my progress opening up to my psychic abilities. The surrender meditation cleared out feelings of attachment, loss, and doubt and replaced them with a loving detachment, a feeling of rich connection to everything around me.

So, what did I do? Well, I was just out of college at the time and in the prime of my life. I was afraid these experiences were pulling me too much away from experiencing an ordinary life. I didn't feel completely human anymore because I no longer cared for human things. Basically, I got scared and asked God to let me live a normal life for a while.

My abilities remained, but I had to really focus to use them. My skills remained a wonderful tool in my life, but the trend toward spiritual asceticism faded. I eventually found a balance between spirit and daily life, and my spiritual life moved back to being a focus of my life.

We have chosen to be human beings for a reason, and our spiritual practice needs to honor our humanity. We resonate with our reality. If we were meant to be angels or some other form of consciousness, then we wouldn't be human beings.

The second thing I learned was there was no need for me to be as black and white as I'd been about practicing the surrender meditation. Prior to discovering the surrender meditation, I floated between two extremes: meditate and stop living a normal life, or stop meditating and be "normal." I could have done both, and engaging more in everyday life prior to traveling so far down my spiritual path could have helped me keep everything in perspective. I was in a rush to grow spiritually and lost perspective on how the material and spiritual are one and the same.

Years passed, and my spiritual and material lives became integrated into just "my life." I'd do psychic readings for friends, and use my intuition as a guide and my ability to see auras to help me understand other people's motivations. I applied my interest in spirituality to land conservation and helped save a lot of land from development. I figured this allowed Nature spirits to have a lot of room in which to play and be happy.

After starting my business, however, my stress levels increased quite a bit, and I decided yoga and meditation could really help me stay focused and centered during the chaotic experience of building a business from the ground up.

About a year later while attending a yoga retreat, I re-experienced the same feeling of surrender and bliss I'd had all those years before. The spontaneous surrender experience happened at a shrine operated by a woman who calls herself Sai Ma. During a break between yoga sessions I visited her shrine. There was a lot of light, sparkly energy throughout the property but so much thicker around the shrine, like a white fog filling the room. I felt compelled to lie down and meditate.

A female presence filled the room with a golden light. She did not feel human to me. She was enormous and wispy and appeared like living gold to my eyes. She smiled down on me. I opened my eyes, and the room was still foggy, the energy was so thick. At the ceiling of the yurt I was in, there was a round opening to the sky. An enormous amount of white light poured out into the sky from the hole. The spirit-woman's golden energy left the yurt as white light. The vision was breathtaking.

My heart filled with the same ecstatic joy I'd felt in my twenties, and I couldn't stop smiling. I surrendered to the joy and let it fill me until we had to return to the workshop. For the rest of the day I couldn't stop smiling, and the golden light stayed with me for hours.

The exercise below is my attempt to explain how to perform the surrender meditation. The closest thing I can find to a similar feeling is the practice of Latihan, a type of meditation practiced by adherents of Subud. I've included a link to further information about Subud in the Recommended Reading.

Exercise:
Surrender Meditation

As usual, find a relaxing, safe place to meditate. Sit, kneel, lie on the ground, hold the Child's Pose if you know yoga, or any other comfortable position. Wear loose-fitting, comfortable clothing. Clear any obstacles away from you, including little things like candles, houseplants, or other objects. You may end up doing a lot of movement.

The surrender meditation has a beginning and an end. The point of the exercise is to just surrender to the moment and see what happens. The process of surrendering works best if you know how to quiet your thoughts, as otherwise you may think about what to do next instead of just letting the process flow. The goal is surrender. Surrender to spirit, surrender your everyday self and blend into the infinite love around you. Allow everything else to melt away, including thoughts, feelings, physical sensations, expectations, memories, sounds, smells, or anything else keeping you tied to the present moment.

When you are ready to start, perform the Owning Your Space exercise from chapter 1, followed by the Heart Breath exercise. When you have finished these and are ready to begin the surrender meditation, assume whatever position you've decided to start with and say or think, "Begin." Telling yourself to begin allows the process to commence. Be completely present without thinking a thing and just breathe into and out of your heart. Anytime you feel distracted, simply say, "I surrender" and bring your attention back to the moment. Bring your awareness to your heart center as you breathe if you feel distracted or not in the moment. The surrender process stems from the heart center, and tuning in to your heart helps break your connection to self and fully fall into the moment.

Many people seem to make noises at first, whether animalistic, gurgling, moaning, or other types of sounds. I believe the noises and other intense experiences are part of a clearing process happening to rid the body-spirit of heavier vibrations stuck in the auric field. The surrender meditation is a very effective method of purification. The entire sequence of events is unique for everyone, but I definitely have noticed those who think about the practice prevent the feeling of full surrender from occurring. And the activity is different for everyone, and different for the same person throughout their life. I've had sessions where I sit still the entire time and other sessions where I am on my feet spinning like a top for four hours. The beauty of surrender is there are no rules; eventually surrender deepens beyond the point of thought, and you enter the state of bliss. No matter how long the sessions, I always feel energized and complete afterward.

I recommend performing the surrender meditation for around fifteen minutes. It can be pretty intense afterward, even if it doesn't feel like anything happened at the time. The body needs time to build up endurance for the surrender process. However, continue practicing until you feel ready to stop; the time limit is just a guide. Always follow your intuition and physical body-wisdom as to how best to proceed. Repeat the exercise as often as you feel like; again, just be sure to check in with your intuition for how much is too much. As mentioned above, I've always felt energized afterward, but it may be different for you, so listen to your body.

The initial clearing process lasts for weeks or months depending on the person. Again, surrender meditation is a very personalized process, and timeframes are merely reference guides. Your body may spontaneously move, which is also a normal part of the process. At first my arms flapped around like a bird and my head bobbed back and forth. In the moment, there was no thinking, and everything just flowed from one movement to the next.

Surrender meditation is a very dynamic practice. The barking and coughing fits gave way to more gentle and loving energies. In concert with the surrender meditation becoming an integral part of my life, many patterns in my life changed. The surrender meditation affects each of us differently, but the trend is that the surrender meditation clears your energy field and brings you into a more refined and loving state of being. Things you once cared so much about won't matter, and new things fill your heart. Change comes effortlessly, and you eventually feel extremely happy to be alive.

The body movements changed from a ground-based pattern to one where I went from my sitting starting pose to standing. There was lots of spinning, spontaneous mudras (hand gestures), and endless and intense feelings of bliss. During the meditation I was visited and cared for by my guides. They spontaneously appeared to assist in the cleansing and rejuvenation that surrender meditation provides.

Surrender meditation is an incredibly cleansing psychic experience. Time has no meaning, and hours pass in what feels like moments. My endurance for the practice carried over to endurance in my life. I was less stressed and more centered, but I also felt stronger. I could hold yoga poses easily for long

*periods of time. I gave up certain habits and adopted new
ones, such as moving to a more vegetarian eating regimen. No
thought influenced these changes; they just happened.*

*I practiced several times a week for several hours at a
time. The process felt so good. My spirit guides knew when I
was ready to practice again and were always there waiting
for me to be begin my next session. Remember the practice of
heart meditation? Well, surrender meditation is heart meditation on a massive scale. My entire house was filled with
positive energy. The experience brought the spiritual into the
everyday world.*

*Surrender meditation is one of the most unusual and
powerful things I've ever experienced, and I wish the process
was easier to describe. All I can say is you'll know it when
you feel it, and until then keep being present to the intention
of "I surrender." Surrender and release of the everyday self
is the key to everything. Upon effectively surrendering, you
feel a buildup of joy, merge with your higher self, learn to
deeply see what is really happening around you, and basically feel great. Aspects of your personal life that once seemed
so important fall away as illusory attachments.*

Life really is very simple, meant to be joyful and easy—a
playground shaped by our intentions and desires. I felt I had access to the most real and present connections to my guides,
their teachers, angels and archangels, but everything was just as

it was supposed to be, so I had no questions for them. I felt completely at peace with myself and the world. Everything made sense: my guides showed me how all the positive and negative aspects of life work together to harmoniously inspire humanity to choose love more and more through time.

Conclusion

Psychic Is the New Normal

*Always know and remember that you are more
than your physical body.*
—ROBERT MONROE

Congratulations! You finished the book! If you can work with the practices in *The Way of the Psychic Heart*, you'll be well on your way to learning anything else you might want to learn from your own higher self and spirit guides. You have embodied everything you need to know to activate a strong spiritual life and grow into your psychic abilities. Your progress will continue at its own perfectly timed pace over the rest of your life. Do not worry if certain exercises don't come to you right away. Keep practicing, and over time you will learn to access everything on your own time in your own way. You will become a much happier and heart-centered person.

I hope this book has helped you experience your spiritual gifts firsthand. Psychic abilities are part of a truly realistic and practical way of living life in the everyday world. I hope you see the benefit of living a heart-centered life full of positive energy, affirmations, and life experiences. With diligent practice, the heart-breathing exercise naturally progresses into the surrender meditation exercises we just learned, so if you're having trouble jumping in to the surrender meditation, then the Heart Breath exercise from chapter 1 is a great alternative.

Staying Heart Centered

The more you practice a heart-centered psychic opening, the more protected you feel. The Owning Your Space exercise is a valuable asset, but down the road your intention alone can clear negative energy from a place. If you ever feel unsafe, however, you can always implement the Owning Your Space and Heart Breath exercise from chapter 1. These two exercises combine to flood a space with your intentions and positive vibrations, and chase away the negative energy.

And the more you practice, the greater your spiritual athleticism will progress, too. Your spiritual life and material life help each be successful. A great way to gauge how your spiritual life is moving along is by observing how these two aspects of yourself, the spiritual and material, flow together. When aligned, your spiritual growth will steadily increase, and your daily life will feel easier. Work feeds your soul, and your soul feeds your work. When these parts of yourself conflict, follow your spiritual guidance to find a new material situation. Our material lives follow our spiritual inclinations, never the other way around. We are spirit-in-flesh, not merely flesh. The material world is the child, and spirit is the parent. Follow the parent's advice, and you'll enjoy your material life much better. A good relationship with yourself makes implementing the principles of the spiritual athlete easier. You will naturally want to be a Good Householder and take care of your daily responsibilities.

The exercise Helping the Body Integrate Spiritual Energy in chapter 2 is also a great segue into the surrender meditation from the last chapter. Becoming comfortable with the flow of energy in your body helps you feel where heart-surrender occurs. It is up to you to follow or not.

All of these experiences maximize your experiences learning the three pillars of psychic development: becoming more aware, learning to see energy, and developing your intuition. In a way, these can be thought of as feeling, seeing, and hearing energy. From these three talents everything else follows. There are many other exercises beyond the ones covered in *The Way of the Psychic Heart* and those will be covered in a future book. For now, enjoy strengthening your skills by practicing the exercises in this book.

As your skills grow and develop, you may spontaneously manifest other abilities not mentioned here. If you have any questions about such things, please feel free to contact me. I'm happy to answer your questions.

Some of these more advanced skills include conscious dreaming, automatic writing, and learning to meet and partner with your spirit guides. These three practices help us keep in touch with our heart-centered path by aligning ourselves with our spirit guides in different media: dreams, channeling, and direct contact. Our guides are our best allies on the path of spiritual awakening, and I chose to highlight particular skills to help you get to know them and work with them. Getting to know these beings can lead to some truly incredible life moments.

Living a Spiritual Life

As you continue walking down your unique and custom-crafted spiritual path, be mindful of the different influences around you. You can consciously choose the path of the heart and stay in alignment with your higher self and your guides. Remember to regularly seal up your energy field to avoid allowing unwanted influences into your spiritual being, and regularly check in with your intuition and your spirit guides for wisdom about the path of your life and how to bring your life more in line with a heart-centered lifestyle.

Doing so increases the power and clarity of your intentions. With time your intentions always happen, although as we learned in chapter 10, the form they take may not be what we imagined. Learning to surrender your conditional intentions for more open-ended, heartfelt requests can help you avoid a lot of unnecessary stress.

Finally, the exercises in *The Way of the Psychic Heart* are specially designed to encourage our spiritual hearts to open wide. We can be a blessing in the world by bringing greater joy and happiness to everything we encounter. Psychic development is a lengthy, lifelong process, however, so remember to give yourself a break if you aren't always successful in your efforts to grow. Every effort you make to grow as a person, to walk the spiritual path and engage your psychic abilities, transforms you into a more heart-centered person. Embrace the pace of your own growth and understand you are not racing to a finish line. The journey is the reward.

I am excited to share what I have learned with those who are interested in such things. I welcome any feedback, alternate techniques, and accounts of your personal experiences. I realize some people have no desire to make love the center of their life and have other reasons to seek spiritual awakening. The saying "All roads lead to Rome" applies to you; if you follow the path long enough, you'll find love at the center. There are many levels to these practices, and I hope you find a place that resonates with your own spiritual journey.

If I may be of any further assistance, please contact me and I will answer your questions to the best of my ability.

Sincerely,

Chad Mercree
February 9, 2013

Recommended Reading

I've found the following list of books helpful on my journey of spiritual awakening. May they be just as helpful for you.

Alli, Antero. *Angel Tech*. Phoenix, AZ: Falcon Press, 1986.

Batie, Howard F. *Healing Body, Mind & Spirit*. St. Paul, MN: Llewellyn Publications, 2003.

Bennett, John G. *Concerning Subud*. London: Hodder & Stoughton, 1958.

Brennan, Barbara Ann. *Hands of Light*. New York: Bantam, 1987.

Butera, Robert. *The Pure Heart of Yoga*. Woodbury, MN: Llewellyn Publications, 2009.

Chia, Mantak. *Awaken Healing Energy through the Tao*. Santa Fe, NM: Aurora Press, 1983.

Coelho, Paulo. *The Alchemist*. San Francisco: HarperSanFrancisco, 1993.

Dale, Cyndi. *Kundalini: Divine Energy, Divine Life*. Woodbury, MN: Llewellyn Publications, 2011.

Diamond, Harvey. *Fit for Life*. New York: Warner Books, 1985.

Hittleman, Richard. *Yoga 28 Day Exercise Plan*. New York: Bantam Books, 1969.

McElroy, Mark. *Lucid Dreaming for Beginners*. Woodbury, MN: Llewellyn Publications, 2007.

Nicoll, Maurice. *Psychological Commentaries on the Teachings of Gurdjieff & Ouspensky*. Boston: Shambhala Press, 1985.

Northrup, Christiane. *The Subtle Body*. Boulder, CO: Sounds True, Inc., 2009.

Ouspensky, P. D. *The Fourth Way*. New York: Vintage Books/Random House, 1957.

Pitchford, Paul. *Healing with Whole Foods*, 3rd edition. Berkeley, CA: North Atlantic Books, 2002.

Rinpoche, Tenzin Wangyal. *Awakening the Sacred Body*. New York: Hay House, 2011.

———. *The Tibetan Yogas of Dream and Sleep*. New York: Snow Lion Publications, 1998.

Tompkins, Peter, and Christopher Bird. *The Secret Life of Plants*. New York: Harper and Row, 1973.

Trungpa, Chogyam. *Shambhala: The Sacred Path of the Warrior*. Boston: Shambhala Press, 1988.

To Write to the Author

If you wish to contact the author or would like more information about this book, please write to the author in care of Llewellyn Worldwide Ltd. and we will forward your request. Both the author and publisher appreciate hearing from you and learning of your enjoyment of this book and how it has helped you. Llewellyn Worldwide Ltd. cannot guarantee that every letter written to the author can be answered, but all will be forwarded. Please write to:

Chad Mercree
⁒ Llewellyn Worldwide
2143 Wooddale Drive
Woodbury, MN 55125-2989

Please enclose a self-addressed stamped envelope for reply,
or $1.00 to cover costs. If outside the USA, enclose
an international postal reply coupon.

Many of Llewellyn's authors have websites with additional information and resources. For more information, please visit our website at http://www.llewellyn.com.

GET MORE AT LLEWELLYN.COM

Visit us online to browse hundreds of our books and decks, plus sign up to receive our e-newsletters and exclusive online offers.

- **Free tarot readings • Spell-a-Day • Moon phases**
- **Recipes, spells, and tips • Blogs • Encyclopedia**
- **Author interviews, articles, and upcoming events**

GET SOCIAL WITH LLEWELLYN

Find us on
Facebook

www.Facebook.com/LlewellynBooks

Follow us on

www.Twitter.com/Llewellynbooks

GET BOOKS AT LLEWELLYN

LLEWELLYN ORDERING INFORMATION

Order online: Visit our website at www.llewellyn.com to select your books and place an order on our secure server.

Order by phone:
- Call toll free within the U.S. at 1-877-NEW-WRLD (1-877-639-9753)
- Call toll free within Canada at 1-866-NEW-WRLD (1-866-639-9753)
- We accept VISA, MasterCard, and American Express

Order by mail:
Send the full price of your order (MN residents add 6.875% sales tax) in U.S. funds, plus postage and handling to: Llewellyn Worldwide, 2143 Wooddale Drive Woodbury, MN 55125-2989

POSTAGE AND HANDLING
STANDARD (U.S. & Canada):
(Please allow 12 business days)
$25.00 and under, add $4.00.
$25.01 and over, FREE SHIPPING.

INTERNATIONAL ORDERS (airmail only):
$16.00 for one book, plus $3.00 for each additional book.

Visit us online for more shipping options. Prices subject to change.

FREE CATALOG!

To order, call
1-877-
NEW-WRLD
ext. 8236
or visit our
website

Discover *your* Psychic Type

Developing and Using Your Natural Intuition

SHERRIE DILLARD

Discover Your Psychic Type
Developing and Using Your Natural Intuition
SHERRIE DILLARD

Intuition and spiritual growth are indelibly linked, according to professional psychic and therapist Sherrie Dillard. Offering a personalized approach to psychic development, this breakthrough guide introduces four different psychic types and explains how to develop the unique spiritual capabilities of each.

Are you a physical, mental, emotional, or spiritual intuitive? Take Dillard's insightful quiz to find out. Discover more about each type's intuitive nature, personality, potential physical weaknesses, and more. There are guided meditations for each kind of intuitive, as well as exercises to hone your psychic skills. Remarkable stories from the author's professional life illustrate the incredible power of intuition and its connection to the spirit world, inner wisdom, and your higher self.

From psychic protection to spirit guides to mystical states, Dillard offers guidance as you evolve toward the final destination of every psychic type: union with the divine.

978-0-7387-1278-9, 288 pp., 5³⁄₁₆ x 8   **$15.99**

Over 150,000 Sold!

Psychic Development

For Beginners

An Easy Guide to Developing and Releasing
Your Psychic Abilities

WILLIAM W. HEWITT

Psychic Development for Beginners

An Easy Guide to Developing and Releasing Your Psychic Abilities

WILLIAM W. HEWITT

MORE THAN 150,000 SOLD!

You possess a secret power that is just waiting to be harnessed—your natural psychic sense.

This unique book on psychic development offers fast and easy techniques that can be used every day to solve problems, psychically shield yourself from harm, contact your spirit guide, attain superior listening skills, boost your reading comprehension, and even reserve that perfect parking space in advance.

Awaken and develop your innate psychic abilities, and ultimately create the kind of life you have always dreamed of. More than 44 fun and simple activities and 28 case studies in this book on psychic development illustrate the effectiveness of these methods.

978-1-567183-603, 216 pp., 5¼ x 8   **$13.99**

Your
Psychic
Self

A Quick and Easy Guide to
Discovering Your Intuitive Talents

Your Psychic Self
A Quick and Easy Guide to Discovering Your Intuitive Talents
Melissa Alvarez

Ever wondered if you were psychic? Your Psychic Self is designed to help you recognize your natural intuitive abilities and strengthen them to enhance your daily life.

In an easy, conversational tone, professional intuitive Melissa Alvarez shares her own experiences and offers direction for discovering where your skills and interests lie within the psychic and metaphysical worlds.

Good for beginners or as an all-around reference, this guide gives you an overview of the signs of intuition, different kinds of abilities, psychic experiences, and forms of intuitive communication. Understand the types of readers—from psychic detectives to animal communicators—and explore your own connection with spirit beings. Use the practice exercises to develop your abilities and learn how to protect yourself from negative influences.

978-0-7387-3189-6, 264 pp., 6 x 9   **$14.99**

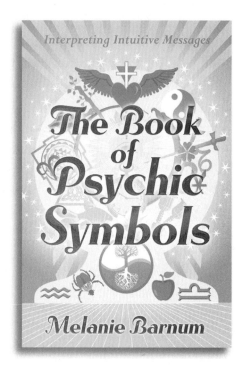

Interpreting Intuitive Messages

The Book of Psychic Symbols

Melanie Barnum

The Book of Psychic Symbols
Interpreting Intuitive Messages
Melanie Barnum

A strong feeling, a remarkable coincidence, a strange dream … What may seem ordinary could actually be an important message—a helpful hint or a warning from a deceased loved one or spirit guide. Open yourself to a wealth of guidance and opportunities by learning how to recognize and interpret the signs and synchronicities all around us.

The Book of Psychic Symbols can help you decode dreams, intuitive flashes, and all psychic impressions. Intuitive counselor Melanie Barnum explains what psychic symbols are, how we receive them, and where they come from. She also shares amazing stories from her life that clarify how the wondrous intuitive process works. In addition to a comprehensive dictionary of 500 symbols, there are many practical exercises for exploring symbols in your life, fortifying your natural intuition, and using psychic symbols to manifest your desires.

978-0-7387-2303-7, 288 pp., 6 x 9   **$15.95**

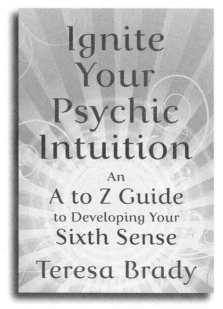

Ignite
Your
Psychic
Intuition

An
A to Z Guide
to Developing Your
Sixth Sense

Teresa Brady

Ignite Your Psychic Intuition
An A to Z Guide to Developing Your Sixth Sense
TERESA BRADY

Developing your psychic powers doesn't have to take a lot of time and patience. Ignite Your Psychic Intuition proves that we can easily tap into our sixth sense, even with the busiest of lifestyles.

In this innovative and easy-to-use guide, Teresa Brady demystifies psychic and intuitive development and step-by-step shows you how to unlock and heighten your extrasensory perception. Designed in an A-to-Z format, this book offers twenty-six practical teaching tools, one for each letter of the alphabet. Discover the four main types of intuitive communication—clairvoyance, clairaudience, clairsentience, and claircognizance—and how to use them to enhance your life.

Beginners and experienced practitioners looking for new ideas will enjoy developing their higher senses through white light bathing, energy scans, salt showers, directed dreaming, chakra cleansing, and crystal gazing.

978-0-7387-2170-5, 288 pp., 5 x 7 $14.95

So You Want to Be a PSYCHIC INTUITIVE?

A Down-to-Earth Guide

Alexandra Chauran

So You Want to Be a Psychic Intuitive?
A Down-to-Earth Guide
Alexandra Chauran

Dependable guidance, communication with departed loved ones, helping friends and family—the lifelong rewards of a strong psychic connection are countless. Whether you're a beginner or already in touch with your intuition, this encouraging, conversational, and hands-on guide can help you improve psychic abilities. Featuring illustrative anecdotes and easy exercises, you'll learn how to achieve a receptive state, identify your source of information, receive messages, and interpret coincidences, dreams, and symbols. Step-by-step instructions make it easy to try a variety of psychic techniques and divination, such as telepathy, channeling, spirit communication, automatic writing, and scrying. There's also practical advice for wisely applying your enhanced psychic skills personally and professionally.

978-0-7387-3065-3, 264 pp., 5³⁄₁₆ x 8   **$14.95**

Intuition

For Beginners

Easy Ways to Awaken Your Natural Abilities

DIANE BRANDON

Intuition for Beginners
Easy Ways to Awaken Your Natural Abilities
Diane Brandon

Have you ever known who was calling when the phone rang? Or have you ever made a decision on an absolute whim—and later felt that you made the right choice? Perhaps you've had an immediate good or bad feeling about a person—and then had that instinct confirmed? Most people, whether they acknowledge it or not, have some degree of intuitive ability.

Diane Brandon has spent the past two decades studying and intuitive development. Whether your intuition is naturally accessible or hidden, this comprehensive and approachable text offers strategies to elevate your level of conscious awareness. Dispelling the myths of intuitive and psychic knowledge, Brandon focuses on how intuition can be applied as a tool of empowerment and self-improvement. Get in touch with your inner voice to improve relationships, solve problems, make well-timed decisions, and more.

978-0-7387-3335-7, 312 pp., 5³⁄₁₆ x 8   **$14.99**